# Closing the Vocabulary

As teachers grapple with the challenge of a new, bigger and more challenging school curriculum, at every key stage and phase, success can feel beyond our reach. But what if there were 50,000 small solutions to help us bridge that gap?

In *Closing the Vocabulary Gap*, Alex Quigley explores the increased demands of an academic curriculum and how closing the vocabulary gap between our 'word poor' and 'word rich' students could prove the vital difference between school failure and success.

This must-read book presents the case for teacher-led efforts to develop students' vocabulary and provides practical solutions for teachers across the curriculum, incorporating easy-to-use tools, resources and classroom activities. Grounded in the very best available evidence into reading development and vocabulary acquisition, *Closing the Vocabulary Gap* sets out to:

- help teachers understand the vital role of vocabulary in all learning;
- share what every teacher needs to know about reading (but was afraid to ask);
- unveil the intriguing history of words and exactly how they work;
- reveal the elusive secrets to achieve spelling success; and
- provide strategies for vocabulary development for all teachers of every subject and phase.

With engaging anecdotes from the author's extensive personal teaching experience woven throughout, as well as accessible summaries of relevant research, Alex Quigley has written an invaluable resource suitable for classroom teachers across all phases, literacy leaders and senior leadership teams who wish to close the vocabulary gap.

**Alex Quigley** is an English Teacher and Director of Huntington Research School, York, UK. He can be found on Twitter @HuntingEnglish and blogs at www.theconfidentteacher.com.

# Closing the Vocabulary Gap

## Alex Quigley

Routledge
Taylor & Francis Group

LONDON AND NEW YORK

First published 2018
by Routledge
2 Park Square, Milton Park, Abingdon, Oxon OX14 4RN

and by Routledge
711 Third Avenue, New York, NY 10017

*Routledge is an imprint of the Taylor & Francis Group, an informa business*

*British Library Cataloguing-in-Publication Data*
A catalogue record for this book is available from the British Library

*Library of Congress Cataloging-in-Publication Data*
Names: Quigley, Alex, author.
Title: Closing the vocabulary gap / Alex Quigley.
Description: Abingdon, Oxon; New York, NY: Routledge, 2018. |
Includes bibliographical references.
Identifiers: LCCN 2017053102 (print) | LCCN 2018005169 (ebook) |
ISBN 9781315113272 (ebook) | ISBN 9781138080607 (hbk) |
ISBN 9781138080683 (pbk) | ISBN 9781315113272 (ebk)
Subjects: LCSH: Vocabulary–Study and teaching. | Educational equalization.
Classification: LCC LB1574.5 (ebook) | LCC LB1574.5 .Q54 2018 (print) |
DDC 372.44–dc23
LC record available at https://lccn.loc.gov/2017053102

ISBN: 978-1-138-08060-7 (hbk)
ISBN: 978-1-138-08068-3 (pbk)
ISBN: 978-1-315-11327-2 (ebk)

Typeset in Celeste and Optima
by Deanta Global Publishing Services, Chennai, India

Katy, Freya and Noah,
This book is written for you.
Every word shared between us is a privilege, always.

Mum and Dad,
Thank you for giving me wealth beyond money, love beyond words.

# Contents

# Contents

# Acknowledgements

There are many people I would like to thank for helping inform this book. I would like to thank Katy Gilbert, my unofficial editor, for tolerating my research and long writing spells, as well as giving me feedback and endless support.

I would like to thank Phil Stock, Helen Day, Robbie Coleman, Tom Martell and Geoff Barton, for giving me helpful feedback on the draft of this book, offering me expert ideas and insight. I would also like to thank Dr Arlene Holmes-Henderson for her expertise that helped shape Chapter 3.

There are many colleagues at Huntington School who directly or indirectly helped me with their insights into vocabulary. In particular, it has been a privilege to watch expert teachers (and students) at work, at Huntington and beyond, to help inform my writing.

Thank you to the team at Routledge for their ongoing support and skill in making this book a reality.

But words are things, and a small drop of ink,
Falling like dew, upon a thought, produces
That which makes thousands, perhaps millions, think.
Lord Byron, *Don Juan*, 1819–1824

# 1 | Closing the vocabulary gap

## Problems and solutions

> The ways of words, of knowing and loving words, is a way to
> the essence of things, and to the essence of knowing.
>
> John Donne

How many words do you know?

It can prove a startling question. Though we use words
all day long when talking, and in reading and writing, we
seldom pay much heed to their importance or ask such
questions. We have all accumulated a vast store of vocabulary that is so integral to who we are that we barely notice
it. Though we are indeed experts with words, we underes-
timate how many words we know.

If I said that the typical vocabulary of readers of this
book would be something around 50,000 to 60,000 words,[1]
would that surprise you?

We are surrounded by a vast wealth of words and they
profoundly affect our lives – words we use and receive,
hear and speak. From the cradle to the dinner table, the
classroom to the boardroom, our wealth of words can
determine our status in life. With well over a million words
stuffed into the English language, we cannot know them
all, but with a greater awareness of words – their rich and
complex meanings, uses and even abuses – we can help

our students develop something like the word-hoard of 50,000 words they need to thrive in school and beyond.[2,3,4]

Many a politician has been heard promising to 'close the gap' of social inequality, but seldom can we credit them for doing so. The gaps between the rich and poor in our society are long lasting and deep rooted, with few policies appearing to mitigate the damaging effects for those children who live in poverty. The problem appears too massive and complex, so we voice our concerns and try to make sure our democratic vote counts. In schools, though we cannot bring an end to poverty, we cannot wait for poverty to end either. Instead, we can shrink the complex issues that beset the most vulnerable children in our care and share something that would appear to be insignificant, but what can prove comprehensible, manageable and ultimately transformative for them. We can share with our students a wealth of words.

There are then thousands of small solutions to the damaging inequalities that we observe in our society and in our classrooms, and they can be found in the English dictionary. By closing the vocabulary gaps for children in our classrooms with their peers, we can offer them the vital academic tools for school success, alongside the capability to communicate with confidence in the world beyond the school gates.

We know that a great deal of our vocabulary is learned incidentally and implicitly outside of those gates. This largely subconscious, hidden growth is like a child's physical development. If you are a parent or carer for a child, you barely notice the daily growth, but over time, the size differences are unmistakable. By paying attention to vocabulary growth at the micro level, we can better understand it. If we better understand it, we can go to work cultivating it and in so doing every child will be gifted a wealth of words.

By simply recognising the value of attending to vocabulary development, we can make a start on closing the gaps that exist in our classrooms. Recognition is a first step, but to address the well documented 'attainment gaps' in our schools and classrooms we need to attend to the vocabulary gaps. It is no silver-bullet solution to improving all educational outcomes for our children, but as E. D. Hirsch Jr, notes, vocabulary size is a good proxy for school success, and therefore it proves a good place for us to start:

> Vocabulary size is a convenient proxy for a whole range of educational attainments and abilities – not just skill in reading, writing, listening, and speaking, but also general knowledge of science, history and the arts.
>
> *A wealth of words*, by E. D. Hirsch Jr[5]

## More than just words

Viewing vocabulary as a proxy for learning, or the reading process, is often criticised as being reductive. The play 'Hamlet' is of course much more than the sum of its 30,557 words. And yet, it offers us a way to cut to the quick of the complexity of a child reading a play, or indeed talking like a scientist, or writing like a historian. It can make things simpler for busy teachers, but not simplistic.

We know that too many students fail to access the reading that is integral to the academic curriculum of school. In the face of this failure, closing the vocabulary gap between children's personal word-hoard and the academic vocabulary of school is a realistic, realisable goal. With new, bigger and harder qualifications at every key stage, the demands of academic vocabulary have only increased. From a child who struggles with a textbook in science, to the students simply giving up in an exam, experiencing a vocabulary knowledge deficit in school can prove an insurmountable hurdle.

3

There is a huge amount of evidence to prove that the vocabulary gap begins early, before children even attend school. It then typically widens throughout their time at school, too often hardening into failure at GCSE level and beyond for word-poor children. Evidence shows that, alongside socio-economic status, vocabulary is one of the significant factors that proved relevant to children achieving an A* to C grade in mathematics, English language and English literature.[6] Such achievement, and the failures that are associated with a limited vocabulary, are inextricably linked to a child's home postcode, along with the pay packet and level of academic qualification of their parents.[7]

The evidence of the vocabulary gap proving a crucial factor for school success is comprehensive, but we have not yet properly addressed the issue in our schools. With the new curriculum seeing many children in tears sitting their SATs reading examination in primary school,[8] as well as students in secondary school grappling with more demanding qualifications at GCSE, the issue of literacy and children actually accessing the full breadth of the curriculum is hitting home more than ever.

Are we missing the seemingly small, but potent solutions to the issue of accessing an academic curriculum?

Back in the 1990s, researchers Hart and Risley[9] studied in detail the linguistic lives of 42 families in the United States. After recording the communication between parents and their children (aged between 7 months and 3 years) over a period of 30 months, they shone a light on some shocking findings:

> From birth to 48 months, parents in professional families spoke 32 million more words to their children than parents in welfare families, and this talk gap between the ages of 0 and 3 year – not parent education, socio-economic status, or race – explains the vocabulary and

language gap at age 3 and the reading and math achievement gap aged 10.

> *The achievement gap in reading,* edited by
> Rosalind Horowitz and S. Jay Samuels, p. 151[10]

The vocabulary gap starts early and is more significant than most people would ever consider. The gargantuan statistic of a 30-million word gap should give us pause. Though this does not mean that every family living in material poverty sees children predestined to have an impoverished vocabulary, it does reveal that we should attend to word gaps wherever they may appear.

This relatively small Hart and Risley study has since been replicated with larger groups of children, with voice-recording technology like the 'language environment analysis system (LENA)', being utilised to collate a vast store of 112,000 hours of recordings from more than 750 children. The evidence reiterates the findings that university educated parents talk more to their children than less educated parents and that such talk correlates with later language ability. There are exceptions to such stories that we should seek out, but the trends run deep in our society and they become writ large in depressing statistics about social mobility, or the lack thereof, in England.

The evidence on vocabulary gaps beginning early and proving a crucial factor in later school success stacks up. Evidence has shown that vocabulary size at 25 months accounted for linguistic and cognitive skills at aged 8.[11] Researchers have established the link between orally tested vocabulary at the end of the first year at school in the United States (between 5 and 7 years old) as a significant predictor of reading comprehension 10 years later.[12] The vital importance of talk and language development in the early years is clear. Any politician who talks about the importance of 'social mobility' should begin with early years provision and language development.

5

For every teacher, parent and politician, the evidence about the importance of vocabulary should prove essential reading. Another research study, the 'British Cohort Study', compared the vocabulary skills of thousands of 5-year-olds across a range of social groups, following the group from 1970 and then into their 30s. What were the findings? Predictably, children with a restricted vocabulary at 5 years old were more likely to be poor readers as adults, experience higher unemployment rates and even have more mental health issues.[13] It was also clear from this evidence that children from disadvantaged backgrounds could recognise and name fewer pictures than their more advantaged peers.

Consider that fact for a moment: these 'word poor' children are left unable to describe their world. For our children then, the limits of their vocabulary really do prove the limits of their world. The evidence is stark and sobering. Though teachers' influences are limited to the classroom, we can still help children better develop a vast store of words and unlock the vital academic vocabulary of school.

For every child to leave school with a word-hoard of something like 50,000 words should be our aim. With all of their rich complexity and depth, words make us who we are, and they help us become who we could be. We should want every child under our care to be able to recognise every picture they see, to write their lives, read about their lived reality and to speak into life their very hopes and dreams.

## The vocabulary gap and the academic curriculum

School children in England face the significant challenges of a new curriculum. The matter of a bigger, harder curriculum is of course multi-faceted, with many time-poor teachers feeling disillusioned and without the requisite training to face the issue of helping *every* child succeed.

By defining the problem of the academic challenge more precisely, we can make a start of finding specific solutions.

In 2016, the educational news was awash with anguished tales of students crying in exams, with the offending item proved to be a Key Stage 2 SATs reading examination.[14] It highlighted the challenges our students face. One text alone, see Figure 1.1, included the vocabulary items: 'unearthed', 'drought', 'freshwater oasis', 'parched', 'receding', 'suffocation' and 'extinct' in a single paragraph of what proves a typically academic text.

This is the reading challenge faced by 10- and 11-year-olds. Putting aside the rights and wrongs of such assessments and their uses, there is no teacher, parent or politician, who would disregard the value and importance of reading.

Now, consider the following question that directly conveys the central importance of vocabulary knowledge to confidently read academic texts:

What is the % of words known in a text to ensure reading comprehension?

50%   55%   60%   65%   75%   80%   85%   90%   95%

Take a look back at the 2016 SATs reading extract. Consider for a moment how many words you would expect 10-year-old children, or even many 15/16-year-olds, to confidently know and understand. We know such comprehension of academic texts is the daily work of our students in every classroom. Reading with understanding is indeed vital to success for children in school.

The answer to the percentage of words known in a text to ensure comprehension is a massive 95%. If that percentage surprises you, consider that Dan Willingham, the renowned cognitive scientist, in his book, *The reading mind*, cites evidence that the percentage is *even* higher in many texts for older students: "Still, studies have measured readers' tolerance of unfamiliar vocabulary, and have

Then, in 2005, a team of scientists unearthed thousands of dodo bones in some mud flats in Mauritius. The remains date back to over 4,000 years ago, when the island was suffering from a lengthy drought. The mud flats would have formed a freshwater oasis in an otherwise parched environment. It is thought that most of the animals, while trying to reach the slowly receding waters of the lake, became stuck and died of thirst or suffocation. However, clearly some dodos survived as they did not become extinct until much later.

This discovery is helping to rehabilitate the image of this much-ridiculed bird. The very fact that the dodo was still alive and well on Mauritius 4,000 years after a drought that claimed the lives of thousands of animals is an indication of the bird's ability to survive. The remains are also helping scientists to find out more about the anatomy of the dodo, for example that it was a much slimmer bird than any pictures suggest.

*Figure 1.1* 'The Dead Dodo' – 2016 SATs reading test

estimated that readers need to know about 98% of the words for comfortable comprehension".[15]

If your first answer for the word knowledge required for comprehension was nearer 75%, then consider the following example of a definition that could be encountered by a secondary school student with approximately 75% of the words blacked out to obstruct comprehension:

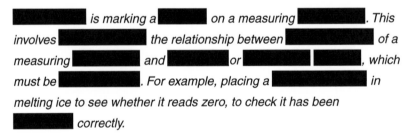

Can you identify what process is being described? If not, how about trying just two words being omitted, thereby making approximately 95% of the words known. Can you identify the missing words and complete the definition now?

██████████ *is marking a scale on a measuring instrument. This involves establishing the relationship between indications of a measuring instrument and standard or reference values, which must be applied. For example, placing a thermometer in melting ice to see whether it reads zero, to check it has been* ██████████ *correctly.*

Now, if you have some scientific knowledge woven together inextricably with your knowledge of academic vocabulary, you will likely make a good job of finding the answer. This example is particularly helpful in revealing that it is the most pertinent words in academic texts that are typically unknown to them. The answer to the example is 'calibration':

> **Calibration** is marking a scale on a measuring instrument. This involves establishing the relationship between indications of a measuring instrument and standard or reference values, which must be applied. For example, placing a thermometer in melting ice to see whether it reads zero, to check it has been **calibrated** correctly.

I have chosen this definition of 'calibration' with intent. It is indeed a specific scientific term related to measurement, but it is also used more broadly to define how we can more carefully assess and adjust something to get it working just right. I have the hope that upon reading this book that teachers in classrooms will be able to better *calibrate* their vocabulary use with students, whilst, crucially, helping students to calibrate their own word knowledge too.

In every classroom explanation, we use vocabulary that will be too difficult, or misunderstood by our children, and so we will need to provide clear, helpful examples. Often, we will do this instinctively, but at other times, we will do it with intent to stretch and grow the knowledge of the children we teach. A good deal of the reading in our classrooms will include vocabulary that is unfamiliar and difficult. Every teacher then needs to be acutely aware of the challenge of academic reading and the teaching tools required to make it accessible.

Being faced with a challenging text is not some rare occurrence, but a daily act in schools. Texts that children encounter in school have an average length of around 85,000 words,[16] including many textbooks. If we take a page 300 words in length, then 95% reading comprehension will leave something like 15 words on the page unclear or unknown. Consider that for a moment. When was the last time you read something but didn't understand such a large number of words? We need to be mindful of how our novice readers in school are grappling with the challenge of academic language. A 10-year-old child who is a good reader will encounter something like 1 million words a year (tantamount to between 10 and 12 short novels). Crucially, approximately 20,000 of those words prove unfamiliar[17] to that child. Given this fact, we quickly recognise how essential it is for our students to have a wealth of words if they are to access the school curriculum.

In subjects like English, children bring a wealth of knowledge around fiction genres and likely patterns of language and sentence structures that they have heard and read since early childhood to help fill in the gaps when their vocabulary knowledge falls below 95%. However, when the same children are faced with non-fiction texts, perhaps a history source, or a science worksheet, they are too often left without years of genre and background knowledge required to understand the text. It is no surprise then that many children make good progress with reading up until about year 5, but then many disadvantaged children can struggle[18] as they face reading more challenging texts. Dan Willingham offers the notion that many disadvantaged children simply do not have the opportunities to develop the background knowledge required to comprehend complex texts. It becomes even harder when young children understand narrative stories in history, science and so on, but then the language switches to something more formal and difficult in non-fiction texts.

For many of our students, they have the lived experience of many more words proving unfamiliar as they travail the challenges of the school day. Struggling daily with reading difficult texts and not understanding words is the harsh reality for many children in our classrooms.

We know that one in five children in England have English as an additional language (EAL students). Though some EAL students can gain a precious linguistic dexterity from being in possession of more than one language, we know that a significant proportion of EAL students experience debilitating vocabulary gaps. It can prove to be simply a practice gap. Children who are learning more than one language, speaking their mother tongue at home, then lack the necessary practice to hone and grow their English vocabulary.

The idioms we can take for granted in English – such as *'the best of both worlds'*, or *'to kill two birds with one stone'* – can prove inscrutable to many EAL children. Consequently, EAL children can exhibit errors in basic phrases and idioms that are part of the fabric of our vocabulary knowledge. Take the sentence I have just written: consider how the metaphor of *'fabric'* is a hurdle for many children. Many of these language barriers and vocabulary gaps can prove invisible even to expert teachers. It leaves some children struggling with the inscrutable language of the classroom, and as a result, school can feel like an alien place.

Despite the known vocabulary gaps described here, explicit teaching of vocabulary is too seldom enacted in our schools. It is likely the result of a lack of training and a related lack of understanding of the importance vocabulary plays in developing reading (this can be true of teachers in every phase of school teaching). Indeed, we know from robust evidence that children with reading difficulties who were exposed to explicit vocabulary teaching benefitted three times as much as those who were not. Not only that, all children benefitted from such vocabulary instruction.[19]

We should then ask:

- How do we explicitly teach vocabulary?
- What training is required for teachers to do so effectively and with confidence?
- How can we more sensitively check for vocabulary gaps in our daily practice in the classroom?

These questions are most pressing as we experience a seismic curriculum shift. The new GCSEs in England have been widely recognised as bigger and harder, with the government heralding the "new, more demanding content".[20] The reality in classrooms is a struggle to help students access these qualifications if they do not possess a wealth of background knowledge and the requisite breadth and depth of academic vocabulary knowledge. We need to ensure that we help our children meet this "demanding content" with the academic tools necessary. Not only that, if we help our students better develop vocabulary, we enrich them with a wealth of words that will serve them well, long after the machinations of yet another curriculum shift has passed into the history books.

So, what exactly is 'harder' about the new curriculum?

New linear qualifications predominantly based on terminal examinations clearly present an increased memory retention demand. Alongside this, the sheer breadth of concepts and topics demands more knowledge and understanding from our students. In Geography GCSE, for example, A-Level concepts have been dropped down into the GCSE curriculum, like the A-Level Mathematics statistical measure, 'Spearman's Rank' being introduced much earlier. Such changes appear to have occurred with scant regard for how such conceptually difficult ideas will be best communicated to younger children. At every year of secondary school, children are routinely reading texts that are considerably beyond their chronological age.

## Remember the 'dead dodo' text!

Teachers are faced with difficult changes given the latest curriculum changes. We are relatively unsupported to teach any differently, so we can **underscaffold** – that is to say, simply getting kids to read harder reading texts earlier, in the hope that mere exposure will convey more mature learning. Conversely, teachers can **overscaffold**, so in English literature, complex literary texts are distilled into gobbets of memorisable passages and quotations. Or in science, the complexity of scientific terms and labels for processes are mediated by bite size PowerPoints and simplified language, with the hope that such simplification will lead to increased understanding over time.

What if the problem isn't simply fitting everything into the curriculum? If we do not ensure our children better understand the very medium of curriculum knowledge and understanding – academic vocabulary – we are stuck in the starting blocks. We are forced to return and reteach language and concepts children did not understand in the first place.

Take the subject of History at GCSE. It is decidedly a bigger and harder qualification than before. Put simply, the history curriculum has shifted from not much more than 100 years of recent history, with topics such as the world wars – with all of their related cultural knowledge still common to us today – to a 1000-year epoch of British history. When faced with a topic such as the Norman Conquest, students encounter unfamiliar vocabulary – such as 'fiefs', 'duchy', 'oaths' and 'relics'. These words require significant background knowledge that is cloaked in religious and social knowledge that is often far removed from their typical background knowledge and their personal word-hoard.

When you add other such challenging historical topics into the History GCSE mix, such as 'Medicine from 1250', there is an increased demand in broad background knowledge and a complex web of academic words. Words like 'plague', 'pandemic' and 'miasma theory' are then pitched alongside the vocabulary that describes historical concepts, like 'causation', 'continuity', 'change' and 'time'. For time, consider just some of the related vocabulary that is needed for understanding: 'ancient', 'mediaeval', 'middle ages', 'modern', 'period', 'reign', 'Anno Domini', 'chronology', 'transitional', 'epoch', 'post-industrial' and 'calendar'. A history teacher then needs to be a skilful teacher of vocabulary alongside supporting children to sift sources for bias and seeking out narratives of continuity and change throughout history.

Where do we start then with the increased challenge of knowledge and understanding of 100 years expanding to 1000 years of history? We know that the degree of complex vocabulary is the biggest factor in determining text difficulty. With a bigger, harder curriculum, in any subject, we begin with the words. When we start with the simplest building blocks of knowledge, we help every student close the vocabulary gap so that they possess the necessary

50,000 words to tackle any epoch of history, any concept in geography and even obscure texts about extinct birds.

Ultimately, every teacher proves a teacher of reading, as it is the primary medium for gaining academic knowledge. For different subjects, reading takes on different purposes and approaches, but broad and deep vocabulary knowledge is always an essential prerequisite for successful reading. Therefore, strategies such as pre-teaching vocabulary, discussing the meaning of words, grouping words, comparing words, finding precise definitions and more, should all prove integral to our classroom practice in our talk, writing and reading.

## Solutions for closing the vocabulary gap

I would ask the question of every teacher reading this book: how do you teach new, unfamiliar vocabulary to children?

For the vast majority of teachers, planned and explicit vocabulary teaching is a rare activity. This integral aspect of communicating with children and teaching academic vocabulary is too often left implicit and invariably something that is *'caught, not taught'*. Vocabulary teaching can be incidental, disorganised and limited, when it needs to be organised, cumulative and rich. If we better adapt our practice to help children to develop their vocabulary, then they'll be better prepared for school success.

As a start, we need then to define our notion of vocabulary more precisely. We all possess two types of vocabulary. First is our **receptive vocabulary** – that is to say, the words we hear and read. Then there is our **expressive vocabulary** – the words we say and write. These are not exactly matched. For example, our reading vocabulary is typically much more complex than the vocabulary we speak. We may understand words as we listen and read, but not know them well enough to use them in our writing.

We know that talk is a well-established solution for developing children's vocabulary. The daily lives of the 'word rich' is characterised by lots of talk around the dinner table, alongside debate and discussion in the classroom. The opposite is of course true, with many children disadvantaged by a lack of talk. Catherine Snow, from Harvard University, has shared evidence showing that a lack of "talk around dinner" inhibited later reading.[21] Surprisingly though, a small number of words predominate in our daily talk. Around 2000 words make up 80% of our spoken language.[22,23] This is important. If we simply encourage talk in the classroom, without a structured approach to using academic language in our talk, it will not develop our children's language. If we know what words are in daily use, we can help our students emblazon their speech with the academic vocabulary that sets them apart for success beyond the school gates.

Of course, the diversity of vocabulary used by a speaker relates to how far we judge a speaker's competence and confidence. Put simply, using an array of academic vocabulary in our talk, drawing upon a vast word-hoard of 50,000 words, helps give not only a confident voice to our students, it also gives others confidence in their voice. That being said, focusing on oracy alone will prove insufficient in developing the vocabulary of our children. We know that even picture books read to children contain many more unique words than typical speech between children in school.[24] Conversations are bound to here and now contexts, using a relatively small number of simple words, whereas reading books opens up experience with language that is considerably more sophisticated, with sentence structures and vocabulary proving much more complex.

Without ignoring the tremendous – indeed, essential – value of oracy, we should be clear: the future success of all of our students rests predominantly on their ability to become proficient and fluent readers. Their capacity to learn, and enjoy learning, is bound inexorably to their reading skill. If they can read it, they can say it. If they can say it with confidence, it provides them a key to success for their future beyond school. Rich, structured talk is a solution to closing the vocabulary gap in our classroom. If this is twinned with high quality reading instruction, then we are well on the way to help children thrive with any curriculum.

## Just get them reading more!

We know just how much reading matters. Most of our vocabulary development is learned incidentally through wider reading, and then incrementally in repeated exposures to those very same words. As we know, a good reader at 10 years old is encountering a million words a year. Encouraging more reading is what Americans call a 'no-brainer'.

A compelling argument is made that the best solution to help develop the vocabulary of children is not to focus on explicit instruction in the classroom, but to simply encourage students to read masses and masses of books for pleasure. It is hard to argue against this proposition and so I won't, but I will say it is not the end of the story.

What we face here is what researcher James Coady termed the 'beginner's paradox'. That is to say, the incidental word learning that happens when reading is important, but without enough knowledge of words, you cannot learn new, related words. We see it every day in the classroom. I have had students in my class begin

17

the year full of energy and effort, but despite my best efforts, their confidence quickly shrinks. The enthusiasm of struggling readers is typically finite and wears off quickly. When you cannot read very well and you have gaps in your vocabulary, reading for pleasure is, well, not very pleasurable.

We come to a well-used Biblical aphorism (Matthew 25:29), put forward by literacy experts like Keith Stanovich[25] and latterly Geoff Barton,[26] called the reading '**Matthew Effect**'. It is from the biblical aphorism: "For unto every one that hath shall be given, and he shall have abundance: but from him that hath not shall be taken away even that which he hath". Put simply, the word rich get richer, but the word poor get poorer.

Some teachers object to explicit vocabulary teaching as a reductive process that does not account for the complexity of learning and reading. Moreover, they put forward the notion that teaching vocabulary somehow supplants the pleasure and power of reading 'naturally'. This is tantamount to saying that you can no longer appreciate the beauty of a rainbow if you are taught about the intricacies of light and the colour spectrum. Teaching vocabulary and reading for pleasure should mutually reinforce one another.

We should promote reading for pleasure every chance we get, but the next time we hear of DEAR (drop everything and read) in a school, we should ask: who is *really* reading? What are they reading? What challenges do they face when reading complex texts? How is their reading enriching their knowledge and helping to grow their vocabulary? We should also help shed any notion that reading a text that is challenging cannot be pleasurable. As the Irish poet W. B. Yeats stated, we should help children revel in the "fascination of what is difficult". Given the challenges of academic vocabulary for older students, this is in fact a necessity.

Encouraging reading for pleasure too often proves an inadequate solution for the vast number of children who do not read fluently and as a consequence read with too little pleasure. Please note what I am not saying. I am not claiming that reading for pleasure lacks value – my entire teaching career is testament to promoting the value of reading and reading for pleasure – but I am proposing the notion that conscious, deliberate attention to word learning is necessary if we are to give every child access to the academic code needed for school success.

We find ourselves moving towards something of a solution in our schools. If we can align, encourage and guide a structured approach to wider reading, alongside a focus on oracy, with *both* being wedded to direct instruction of academic vocabulary and reading, we will get near a solution to the problem of students tackling a bigger, harder curriculum. This approach can and should offer children crucial independent word learning strategies, so that they can read successfully when they encounter new words. These strategies are of huge value for life-long learning far beyond the school gates.

It is the core business of every teacher not just to understand how children learn to read, but also how they read to learn. Early vocabulary learning and reading development is of course essential. I cannot think of a more important act of a healthy society than to help a child learn to read, but the notion that early intervention will automatically sustain learning success later on is insecure. Children are not simply 'fixed at five' (when they typically have learned to read) and then reading takes care of itself. This notion – the so-called 'vaccination model of teaching'[27] – ignores the issue of primary to secondary school transition, that sees too many children unable to make the learning leap to dealing with multiple academic subjects, each with their own specialist background knowledge and vocabulary.

Knowledge of how children 'learn to read', and then go onto 'read to learn', is essential for *every* teacher.

We need to cultivate '**word consciousness**' in every child. This describes how we notice words and are interested and curious about them. It can help make the unfamiliar academic vocabulary of school accessible to every child. Take the word '*circle*'. How many students, or teachers for that matter, consider digging down into the etymological roots of the word – its rich linguistic history? Knowledge of **etymology** is complemented by knowledge of word parts – known as **morphology**. Hidden in the roots of '*circle*' is the Greek word part 'cycl', meaning circle. This word part is found in related words: such as 'recycle', 'bicycle', 'cyclone', 'encyclopaedia', 'tricycle' and 'motorcycle'. Recognising parts of words relate in word families helps our children to develop deeper word knowledge that helps accelerate the growth of their vocabulary.

An important point here is that we must give our students the necessary tools to develop their vocabulary independently. Considering we want a child leaving school to have something like 50,000 words, it is a daunting task. But we can close the gap. By explicitly teaching a mere few hundred words well in the classroom, children grow their vocabulary exponentially by learning the related word families and having more tools to read independently with success. Children can go on to learn around 3000 to 4000 words annually. Year upon year of such growth sees the 50,000 figure become achievable for each child we teach.

Attention to children developing their vocabulary should become a part of school and teacher planning in schools. We can take the following steps, supported by this book:

1  Train teachers to become more knowledgeable and confident in explicit vocabulary teaching.
2  Teach academic vocabulary explicitly and clearly, with coherent planning throughout the curriculum.
3  Foster structured reading opportunities in a model that supports students with vocabulary deficits.
4  Promote and scaffold high quality academic talk in the classroom.
5  Promote and scaffold high quality academic writing in the classroom.
6  Foster 'word consciousness' in our students (e.g. sharing the etymology and morphology of words).
7  Teach students independent word learning strategies.

Word learning and reading development is a complex issue and as such it requires complex, expert solutions. We can do it better and assess and evaluate our impact as we do it. In seeking to close the vocabulary gap, we exhibit our care and high aspirations for each and every student we teach. It is an aspiration shared by the genius linguist and author David Crystal:

Education is the process of preparing us for the big world, and the big world has big words. The more big words I know, the better I will survive in it. Because there are hundreds of thousands of big words in English, I cannot learn them all. But this doesn't mean that I shouldn't try to learn some.

*Words, words, words,* by David Crystal, p. 124

## IN SHORT…

- Being in a word-poor context at a young age can have far-reaching negative consequences for our children. A restricted vocabulary as a young child goes on to correlate with factors in later life such as employment, pay and even health and wellbeing as an adult.
- We need to make the hidden process of vocabulary development visible.
- The explicit teaching of vocabulary can enrich children's knowledge and understanding of the world *and* vocabulary is a useful proxy for a great deal of general knowledge in a range of subject domains.
- By explicitly teaching a mere 300 to 400 words a year we can foster an annual growth of around 3000 to 4000 words. From reception to leaving school, we can therefore help children develop an essential word-hoard of something like 50,000 words.
- The challenges of the new academic curriculum in England are related to an increase in reading comprehension demand. Complex academic vocabulary is one of the biggest drivers when it comes to an increased degree of difficulty in the new curriculum in primary and secondary schools in England.
- Supporting children to read more is vital to helping them grow their vocabulary, but we need to ensure that we better teach reading and not rely solely on 'reading for pleasure'. We should encourage children to read broadly for pleasure, whilst immersing children in word-rich classrooms that have a focus on vocabulary development.

# Notes

1 How word knowledge is measured and what is considered to constitute knowing a word influences vocabulary size estimates. The following article is an interesting overview of the literature on vocabulary size, offering a small study that poses a lower average vocabulary size for UK university undergraduates of around 10,000 words: Treffers-Daller, J., & Milton, J. (2013). 'Vocabulary size revisited: The link between vocabulary size and academic achievement'. *Applied Linguistics Review*, 4 (1): 151–172. doi: 10.1515/applirev-2013-0007.
2 Graves, M. F. (2005). *The vocabulary book: Learning and instruction (language and literacy series)*. New York, NY: Teachers College Press.
3 Nagy, W. E., & Herman, P. A. (1987). 'Breadth and depth of vocabulary knowledge: Implications for acquisition and instruction'. In M. McKeown & M. Curtis (eds.), *The nature of vocabulary acquisition* (pp. 19–35). Hillside, NJ: Lawrence Eelbaum Associates.
4 Crystal, D. (2007). *Words, words, words*. New York, NY: Oxford University Press.
5 Hirsch Jr, E. D. (2013). 'A wealth of words. The key to increasing upward mobility is expanding vocabulary'. *City Journal*, 23 (1). Accessed online on 20 October 2016 at: www.city-journal.org/html/wealth-words-13523.html.
6 Spencer, S., Clegg, J., Stackhouse, J., & Rush, R. (2017). 'Contribution of spoken language and socio-economic background to adolescents' educational achievement at aged 16 years'. *International Journal of Language Disorders*, 52: 184–196. doi: 10.1111/1460-6984.12264.
7 Spencer, S., Clegg, J., & Stackhouse, J. (2012). 'Language and disadvantage: A comparison of the language abilities of adolescents from two different socioeconomic areas'. *International Journal of Language and Communication Disorders*, 47: 274–284. doi: 10.1111/j.1460-6984.2011.00104x.
8 Ward, H. (24 May 2016). TES online. 'Try the SATs reading paper that left pupils in tears'. Accessed online on 27 May 2016 at: www.tes.com/news/school-news/breaking-news/try-sats-reading-paper-left-pupils-tears.
9 Hart, B., & Risley, T. (1995). *Meaningful differences in the everyday experience of young American children*. Baltimore, MD: Paul H. Brookes Publishing.

10  Horowitz, R., & Samuels, S. J. (2017). *The achievement gap in reading: Complex causes, persistent issues, possible solutions.* New York, NY: Routledge.

11  Marchman, V. A., & Fernald, A. (2008). 'Speed of word recognition and vocabulary knowledge in infancy predict cognitive and language outcomes in later childhood'. *Developmental Science*, 11: F9–F16.

12  Cunningham, A. E., & Stanovich, K. E. (1997). 'Early reading acquisition and its relation to reading experience and ability 10 years later'. *Developmental Psychology*, 33: 934–945.

13  Law, J., Rush, R., Schoon, I., & Parsons, S. (2009). 'Modeling developmental language difficulties from school entry into adulthood: Literacy, mental health, and employment outcomes'. *Journal of Speech, Language and Hearing Research*, 52 (6): 1401–1416.

14  Department of Education, UK Government (2016). *The way of the Dodo.* London: Department of Education. Adapted from an article in the *London Evening Standard* by Ben Gilliland.

15  Willingham, D. T. (2009). *Why don't students like school?* San Francisco, CA: Jossey Bass.

16  Nagy, W. E., & Anderson, R. C. (1984). 'How many words are there in printed school English?' *Reading Research Quarterly*, 19: 304–330.

17  Oakhill, J., Cain, K., & Elbro, C. (2015). *Understanding and teaching reading comprehension.* London: Routledge.

18  Willingham, D. T. (2017). *The reading mind: A cognitive approach to understanding how the mind reads.* San Francisco, CA: Jossey Bass, p. 128.

19  Elleman, A., Linda, E., Morphy, P., & Compton, D. (2009). 'The impact of vocabulary instruction on passage level comprehension of school-age children: A meta-analysis'. *Journal of Educational Effectiveness*, 2: 1–44.

20  'OFQUAL guidance: "Getting the facts"'. (2014). Accessed online on 1 February 2017 at: www.gov.uk/government/publications/get-the-facts-gcse-and-a-level-reform/get-the-facts-gcse-reform.

21  Snow, C. E., & Beals, D. E. (2006). 'Mealtime talk that supports literacy development'. *New Directions for Child and Adolescent Development*, Spring (111): 51–66.

22  Carter, R., & McCarthy, M. (2006). *Cambridge grammar of English: A comprehensive guide. Written and spoken English.* Cambridge: Cambridge University Press.

23 O'Keefe, A., Carter, R., & McCarthy, M. (2007). *From corpus to classroom: Language use and language teaching.* Cambridge: Cambridge University Press, p. 32. Accessed online on 5 May 2017 at: http://npu.edu.ua/!e-book/book/ djvu/A/iif_kgpm_OKeefee.%20FCTC.pdf.

24 Massaro, D. W. (2016). 'Two different communication genres and implications for vocabulary development and learning to read'. *Journal of Literacy Research,* 47 (4): 505–527.

25 Stanovich, K. E. (1986). 'Matthew effects in reading: Some consequences of individual differences in the acquisition of literacy'. *Reading Research Quarterly,* 22: 360–407.

26 Barton, G. (2013). *Don't call it literacy! What every teacher needs to know about speaking, listening, reading and writing.* London: Routledge.

27 Shanahan, T., & Barr, R. (1995). 'Reading recovery: An independent evaluation of the effects of an early instructional intervention for at risk learners'. *Reading Research Quarterly,* 30 (4): 958–996.

# 2 What every teacher needs to know about reading

James would stand out in my year 9 English class from lesson one. If the group were working away with quiet industry, he would be scanning the room, seeking out partners in distraction. His reputation in school had quickly hardened: 'silly', 'immature', 'not the academic type' – even downright 'naughty'.

Tackling the reading of Shakespeare or Dickens proved a challenge for most students; the elaborate word choices were like inscrutable relics for students like James. One lesson, early in the year, I sat down with a copy of Dickens' *A Christmas carol*, before asking James to read from a well-thumbed page. He began, quietly and tentatively, reading aloud each word. His bravado drained away and his reading issues were quickly held in sharp relief with each word he slowly uttered. Quick, uncertain looks betrayed his emotions.

Students like James navigate through school with a crafty skill: that of avoiding reading and masking gaps in their knowledge and a damaging vocabulary deficit. After what must have proved a daily trial at primary school, they bounce from one lesson to another in secondary school, each subject proving a new and unfamiliar language to them.

Each lesson that James doesn't quite grasp what he has read, or fails to communicate with the tools of academic vocabulary, he suffers a near imperceptible loss. Over time, those losses accumulate and harden into failure.

## The trouble with reading

In assigning a title to this chapter, 'What every teacher needs to know about reading', I could have easily added in parenthesis: 'but were afraid to ask'. A curious fact about the teaching profession in England is that despite reading proving a foundational skill for **all** learning, many teachers would struggle to explain how children 'learn to read' and how they then go on to 'read to learn'.

My personal experience as an English teacher – a teacher of reading, no less – is that I am pretty much self-taught. Cobbling together a working knowledge of how children read, and doing so by chance, is quite clearly an ineffective model that fails both teachers and children. We would not expect a doctor to walk into a hospital surgery and whip out some pliers ready to begin surgery on the basis of some basic anatomy training and binge-watching a series of Casualty. Every teacher is a teacher of reading and every teacher is a teacher of academic vocabulary. They are the most vital tools for learning that our children possess. Our approach as a profession should reflect these most basic of truths.

Would most year 6 teachers be able to help a young child who could not yet read with confidence? Would the majority of GCSE Chemistry teachers, by way of example, be able to easily support a struggling child-like James to read and to access the uniquely complex vocabulary of chemistry? The likely answer is no. And yet, as Dan Willingham rightly states, "teaching content is teaching reading". Word knowledge proves to be essential for our knowledge of the world and in every domain – from chemistry to computer science, and many more – it is of crucial importance.

What you are doing as a reader of this book is building a '**mental model**'. You are piecing together the gist of the topic of vocabulary, reading, teaching and learning. Happily, you bring a wealth of words and background knowledge to your reading. Having read so much in school, university, professionally and beyond, you bring an intuitive model of non-fiction texts, their structure (headings, quotations, diagrams), their word choices, codes and conventions. When faced with a new, unfamiliar word, you'll be able to comfortably infer from the related information the meaning, or you could quickly scan a reference or web search for some more answers. It all feels, well, so *easy* to the expert adult reader.

When we deconstruct the seemingly intuitive act of reading into its component parts, we can note that for most of our novice students, what is required for a confident '*mental model*' of the text is not automatic or natural. Weak readers lack the vocabulary and understanding of genre that we can take for granted. Weak readers do not have the background knowledge to connect unfamiliar words to what they already know (the necessary "mental Velcro" as described by E. D. Hirsch, Jr). Weak readers do not have enough knowledge to do quick research to repair gaps in what they know. They most often do not even know what they don't know!

The 'vocabulary gap' then is a useful proxy for the knowledge and understanding of strong readers compared to our weaker, novice readers. Novice status can well describe many of the 5-year-old children we teach, but also many 15-year-old children too. With a fifth of school children in England learning English as an additional language, we need to pay more heed to teaching the fundamental aspects of reading.

We know that if children leave school with weaknesses in reading that it has a damaging effect on their wellbeing, career prospects and even their physical and mental health. With this in mind, Mark Seidenberg argues that: "An introductory course in linguistics should be a permanent requirement for teaching children. Educators need to know how language works".[1] It is hard to disagree. The very future of children like James depends on the vital act of reading and their ability to know and learn the academic vocabulary of school.

We know that a great deal of our development in reading, and our accumulated store of vocabulary, happens incidentally and implicitly over time. It is invisible to us in the main. Most children and adults do become competent readers and they have great success in growing their vocabulary. But just because many children do learn to read with great success without structured and explicit vocabulary instruction, it does not mean it should prove the de facto position for schooling. Most of the people reading this book won't have studied and developed vocabulary through strategic explicit teaching, but this implicit approach to academic reading presents us with winners and losers. The winners go on to teach and preach how they themselves succeeded, but the losers are struck dumb, their voices lost to the debate.

You can see this unwitting 'curse of the expert' in the classroom. A teacher who has lived with a wealth of academic words can teach geography or mathematics and, however well-meaning, speak with the assumption that the complex words that they use, from 'deciduous' to 'decimal', are likely known by many of the students in their class. Unwittingly, we can easily miss the subtle vocabulary gaps of many of our students.

Every teacher is busy and beset by the job of keeping up with changes in the curriculum, wrestling with their own subject knowledge, as well as planning, marking and much more. Still, having a deep understanding of how children learn to read, and go on to read to learn, is quite simply too important to leave to chance. We know that teachers with more explicit knowledge of reading development do a better job of teaching early reading skills,[2,3,4] so the rewards for our efforts in knowing more about reading are well within our grasp.

In the rest of this chapter, I am to shrink the complexity of reading – one of the most sophisticated and brilliant of cognitive processes – down to something I hope is clear and useful for every teacher, regardless of the subject, stage or age of children that they teach. Some of the language used to describe reading is rather inevitably worthy of a course in introductory linguistics, and yet, it should without doubt prove a part of the vocabulary of every teacher.

## What we know about the teaching of reading

We know an awful lot about reading. Literacy is one of the most researched topics on the planet, and the corrosive influence of illiteracy is still an international issue that politicians and teachers are struggling to eradicate the world over. In England, though we are one of the world's wealthiest nations, we see older age groups of people (from 55 to 65 years of age) outperform our youngsters (16 to 18 years of age) in literacy measures[5] for the first time in decades.

In modern history, as our IQ is seemingly on a slow but inexorable rise, a decline in literacy should give us cause for concern, as well as strong impetus for action.

The English language is uniquely difficult compared to many other languages. It is known as a '**deep orthography**' (orthography is the spelling system of a language). That is to say, each letter in the English alphabet maps onto lots of different potential sounds. For example, the 'sh' sound – or **phoneme** – can be found with many spelling variations: <u>sh</u>ell, fi<u>sh</u>, spe<u>ci</u>al, sta<u>ti</u>on, cap<u>ti</u>on, pa<u>ss</u>ion and <u>s</u>ugar.

In contrast, in languages with a '**shallow orthography**', such as Finnish, sounds and spellings are very consistent and a letter maps directly to a consistent single sound.

For our beginning readers then, the act of reading in English proves a particularly tough challenge. Wedded to the difficulty inherent in the English language is how the reading brain combines an array of processes woven together with startling intricacy. Each interconnected component means that you cannot teach any one aspect of reading in isolation. Given this fact, although vocabulary knowledge is vital for reading success, we have to recognise that it sits as part of the reading process.

The most helpful analogy for the complex processes of reading is provided by Dr Hollis Scarborough's '**reading rope**', shown in Figure 2.1[6] (you can find this and more in the Education Endowment Foundation 'Improving Literacy at KS2 Guidance Report'[7]).

The '*reading rope*' helpfully describes the two key components of skilled reading: '**word recognition**' (the ability to

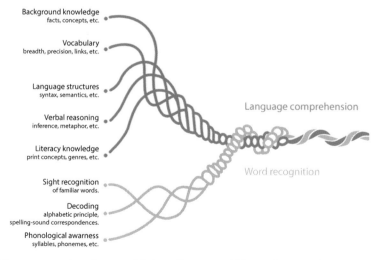

*Figure 2.1*   Scarborough's 'reading rope' (from the EEF 'Improving Literacy at KS2 Guidance Report')

read individual words) and 'language comprehension' (the ability to understand words, sentences, texts and genres). This 'Simple View of Reading' is not something universally understood by teachers. For primary school teachers helping children to learn to read, this is much better known. Yet, for most teachers of older students, where *reading to learn* is predominant, many teachers would struggle to help children to read and comprehend effectively.

For teachers, from Reception class to leaving Sixth Form or college, we are working to help strengthen the 'reading rope' of our children. By paying deliberate attention to vocabulary growth, we provide a focus on reading that is essential to all learning. It proves an integral thread in the rope and one that we could weave more successfully into our classroom practice with greater knowledge and understanding.

So what does this mean for children like James?

Finding the answers to his poor reading is located in his obvious lack of fluency. James reading a relatively low number of words per minute was not due to an inability to decode. He could sound out individual words with little prompting; however, when faced with the uncommon words in long sentences, so prevalent in the writing of Dickens, his confidence would wane and he would begin to slow and struggle. Just a few questions to probe his understanding of the words used by the writer exposed James vocabulary knowledge gap. He could decode words, sounding them out pretty consistently, but he didn't understand enough of them to devise a 'mental model' of the story. Grappling with a single sentence including 'grindstone', 'wrenching', 'covetous' and 'sinner' stretched James too far beyond his personal word-hoard.

No quick fix is available to James, nor the busy teacher, but knowing his issue with words is a start. Teaching James differently and more effectively is within our reach. Every teacher has students like James in their classroom, young or old. We teach EAL students (some remarkably dextrous with their grasp of multiple languages); students with subtle gaps in their knowledge; students with dyslexia and profound language difficulties; students with exceptional language skills far beyond age-related expectations. For these reasons, we are all teachers of reading who need to better understand the process.

## The 'Big Five'

In the United States, back in 2000, a panel of reading experts surveyed the best available evidence on reading to devise the '**Big Five**' – the five crucial components for the effective teaching of reading (see Figure 2.2).[8] It is evidence that remains robust and instructive to us today. Now,

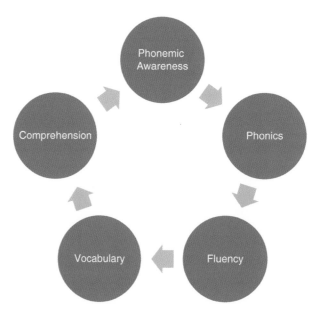

*Figure 2.2*  The 'Big Five' effective components of the effective teaching of reading (from the National Reading Panel Report, 2000)

I will stop short of putting you through an introductory linguistics course, as recommended by Seidenberg, but knowing about the interconnected processes that make up the act of reading is important for every teacher.

## 1 Phonemic awareness

A **phoneme** is the most basic unit of sound in a word. For example, in the word *cat* you have three phonemes: /c/ /a/ /t/. If said cat lapped from a *dish*, then you would have three phonemes that map onto the four letters: /d/ /i/ /sh/. Phonemic awareness then is the knowledge that words are made up of a combination of sounds. It is integral to our ability to learn to read.

This process typically evolves in early reading and you assess phonemic awareness in lots of ways, such as:

- Phonemic identification, for example, what sound is shared in all of the following words? Rule, rude and ripe.
- Phoneme isolation, for example, what is the final sound in the word 'radish'?
- Phoneme deletion, for example, what word is left if you remove 'e' from 'ripe'?
- Phonemic blending, for example, what word is made up of the sounds /sh/ /o/ /p/?

Primary school teachers deploy many of these strategies expertly, but *typically* such strategies are no longer needed once a child develops basic reading fluency (around year 4 for many children). In secondary school, you can observe a modern foreign language (MFL) teacher deploy similar tactics for learning a second language, or a science teacher unlocking a family of words with phonemic awareness, such as exploring how 'alkanes' in chemistry all have an 'ane' ending.

Phonemic awareness provides the foundations for reading – translating speech to the 'alphabetic principle', mapping the corresponding sound (the phoneme) to the letter (the grapheme). Sounding out, blending and segmenting parts of words is a crucial first step to having the tools for successful vocabulary development and reading. Without it, children will struggle to access most facets of an academic curriculum.

For more on phonetic sounds and the 'alphabetic principle', particularly its role in word building and spelling, see Chapter 6.

## 2 Phonics

Phonics is the method of instruction that teaches students to recognise how sounds and letters map onto one another, with all the varied sound and letter correspondences and their tricky variations. With **synthetic phonics**, you take individual sounds, segmenting them, /c/ /a/ /t/, before blending them together into 'cat'. For the '*deep orthography*' of the English language, this is a complex business; 26 letters in the alphabet correspond to 44 sounds, or phonemes. Then in around 144 sound and letter combinations, these building blocks compose the half a million words in the English language.[9] Most words are much trickier than 'cat'!

Invariably, the complex sound system and alphabetic code of English leads to a structured approach to teaching phonics from the start of school, first and fast, in a coherent sequence. A confident grasp of the alphabetic code is a vital foundation for language and vocabulary development. Once mastered, decoding becomes automatic.

Here is a quick phonics glossary to help:

- Blending. The process of identifying the sounds then running them together, for example, /d/ /o/ /g/ becomes 'dog'.
- Digraph. Two letters that together make one sound, for example, /sh/. There are different types of digraph – vowel, consonant and split.
- Split digraph. When a digraph is split by a consonant it becomes a 'split digraph'; for example, in 'wrote', 'oe' is one sound, but it is split by the 't'.
- Grapheme. A letter or group of letters representing one sound (phoneme), for example, 'ck', 'igh', 't' and 'sh'.
- Phoneme. The smallest unit of sound in a word, for example, /p/ in 'pad'.
- Grapheme–phoneme correspondence. The ability to match a phoneme to a grapheme and vice versa.
- CVC. The abbreviation for 'consonant vowel consonant', the most common order of sounds in a word, for example, 'fat'.
- Synthetic phonics. The most common method in English schools for teaching early reading that teaches the letter sounds first, before then teaching children to go on and blend these sounds – phonemes – into words.
- Analytic phonics. The method for teaching early reading that begins with whole words and then recognises common phonemes, such as the /sh/ in 'shot', 'sharp' and 'shave'. It relies heavily on 'phonemic awareness'.

Once a child has learnt to sound out words, they quickly begin to map what words look like, such as letter pairs, common word parts and whole words. Over the months and years of cumulative reading, each child maps out a vast array of sound and letter correspondences. Young children learning to read really is a majestic act of pattern and meaning making we can too easily take for granted.

Children who cannot decode the sounds of words and blend them together confidently will struggle with reading. We see this in the early years of school, but many children in secondary school have issues with decoding that inhibit their progress in pretty much every subject in the curriculum. It is imperative for schools to act in this instance and track reading development with good assessment. Also, crucially, we should expect that every teacher has at least a basic understanding of phonics and how children learn to read.

The best available evidence would indicate that teaching phonics first, and thoroughly, is an efficient and effective approach to developing early reading, but that there is more to reading than just decoding and that reading understanding requires a more complex, deep understanding of language and vocabulary. As the noted linguist Louisa Moats states: "a child cannot understand what he cannot decode, but what he decodes is meaningless unless he can understand it".[10]

Once more, our breadth of vocabulary matters for word decoding because it's easier to decode words you know, or ones that sound *like* words you know.[11]

## 3 Fluency

In the process of reading over and over, the decoding of sounds becomes automatic, like how an experienced driver can drive their car without much conscious mental effort. We can read with good understanding at about four or five words per second. Hypothetically then, we can read a Harry Potter novel – comprising around 77,000 words – in little over four hours.[12] Reading with "speed, accuracy and proper expression"[13] is harnessed through actions at school and in the home, like paired reading, repeated reading and more.

Children can undertake what is known as 'fast mapping', that is to say, recognising words at a momentary glance. Usually though, the challenging academic vocabulary of school requires lots of repeated exposures. As a child practises over time, with more and more reading, they develop *fluency*. It is this reading skill that sees students manage and flourish in exams, reading questions quickly and with understanding, before tackling complex academic texts. The more fluent the child, the more mental energy they can devote to grappling with the more challenging meaning of the text and the vocabulary therein.

By recognising words automatically, fluent readers are able to put expression in their voices, so that reading can sound confident and clear, like '*natural*' speech. Most teachers can quickly pick up on when a child is a fluent reader or not by listening to them read for a short amount of time.

If a child is struggling to read more than 10 words per 100 in a given text, then they are exhibiting a fluency issue that needs addressing. Simple strategies can help children. Rereading is an important strategy to develop fluency. We can ask, when is there an opportunity to read a given text two or three times? Supervised peer reading can offer a safe, practical method for rereading.

If we return to James, we can see his inability to read fluently. He can decode most words, sounding them out, but his fitful, stop-start reading runs aground when he is trying to grapple with rare vocabulary – sounding them out and understanding the meaning of such words. He struggles with how the words fit meaningfully in the sentence, as well as what the author may be stressing as sad, happy or exciting. For James, his lack of fluency results in a reading bottleneck, as his lack of vocabulary knowledge slows him down. If James is reading 'Humbug!' from the mouth of Scrooge, for example, then word knowledge is crucial.

Without understanding vocabulary with some depth too, the appropriate expression is harder to detect.

There is no doubt that the more words you know and understand deeply, the easier it is to develop reading fluency.

## 4 Vocabulary

You didn't think the reading panel would miss out vocabulary did you? Of course, the ultimate aim of reading is comprehension: understanding the meaning of the text. Some children can decode effectively, but they still struggle to comprehend a text because they have specific vocabulary deficits and significant gaps in their background knowledge.

A child could decode 'cracking' and make a sound attempt at the word in common usage, but it takes deeper vocabulary knowledge to know that in chemistry, 'cracking' has a very specific meaning different from common parlance (one that is related to a process in which larger hydro-carbons are broken down into smaller hydrocarbons). Even for many skilled readers of this book – the non-scientists – such depth of word knowledge can be missing.

Deep vocabulary knowledge can help a child navigate a text by making patterns and by differentiating meaning. Once you can decode the word 'break', you then need to develop a deep understanding of how that word works in texts and in 'typical' daily communication. With as many as 70 different meanings (think a 'break' in tennis; to 'break' glass; morning 'break' at school; a 'break-up'; a stress-fuelled 'breakdown' and many more), a single word like 'break' sees us draw upon a vast store of vocabulary knowledge to unlock understanding.

We can be explicitly taught challenging academic vocabulary so that we can attend to its complex meaning. In her book on *Infusing vocabulary into the reading-writing workshop*, Amy Benjamin describes word depth thus:

> To really understand and remember a word, we need to spend some quality time with it, get to know its history and family (etymology), subtleties, synonyms, near-synonyms, antonyms, near-antonyms, spelling and morphological forms (word parts).[14]
>
> *Infusing vocabulary into the reading-writing workshop,* by Amy Benjamin, p. 12

Chapter 3 dives into 'word depth', but hold onto your breath for now.

Even when we are simply enjoying reading, or scanning a story on our phones, we are subconsciously updating our vocabulary store, adding depth of meaning to known words, storing new ones, connecting words, recognising patterns and making meaning.

## 5 Text comprehension

Vocabulary knowledge is essential for reading comprehension success, whilst comprehension is also necessary for developing vocabulary. The ultimate aim of reading is understanding – therefore comprehension is what we are after in the classroom, and beyond, when reading.

John Firth, an esteemed linguist used the aphorism: "you shall know a word by the company it keeps".[15] When we are faced with a new word, we draw upon our knowledge of the words that attend it. This is why vocabulary knowledge is twinned with comprehension strategies like skimming for related word meanings and asking questions when you are uncertain about a word. The more words we know, the easier it is to develop a mental model that coheres the meaning of a given text.

It also reveals the importance of understanding word order to ascertain successful comprehension. Faced with a sentence from a historical source, such as 'he drank from the flagon', a child may have no knowledge of the old-fashioned word 'flagon', but they recognise it is a noun, and the action of drinking from it indicates some approximate understanding of what the word means. Now, the context and grammar of sentences can misdirect children (more on this in Chapter 7), but they invariably offer useful clues for a child struggling to comprehend a text.

The difficulty in comprehending a text does not, of course, just depend on difficulty of the words. Sentence length and complexity, genre, text structure and so on, all contribute in determining whether a text is difficult to read for our students. Many students who can decode word sounds have gaps in their comprehension. Without a broad and deep vocabulary knowledge, students cannot make the appropriate inferences in more difficult texts. Given a sentence with a 'misdirective context' (it is potentially misleading), such as, 'he knew he would relish the opportunity to take the lead', a child with shallow vocabulary knowledge might guess at 'relish' to mean 'take the chance'.

'Poor comprehenders' make up approximately 10% of 7- to 11-year-olds,[16] which means that habitually checking on comprehension is significant in every classroom in primary school. Evidence shows that poor comprehenders can, in many cases, decode words, but their vocabulary knowledge is weak and faced with more complex language, like metaphorical language, they can struggle. Their transition to secondary school can prove difficult, given the sheer range of difficult academic reading.

We know that strategies like helping students to generate questions about their reading, to summarise a text or to use graphic organisers, can help students develop the tools to internalise the strategies of a successful reader. We also know that the more children read, the more they grow their knowledge and understanding of the world. They then bring more background knowledge to any new reading they encounter, asking better questions about what they read, seeing gaps in their own knowledge and more.

Why is all of this relevant to a busy teacher, teaching Biology or Art at GCSE to a class full of children, you may ask?

Too easily, we see our student groups as a homogenous mass. We set homework tasks, or we give them a text related to the topic at hand. Often, we'll spend little time considering the readability of a text we expect every student to read with confidence. Moreover, a seemingly clear explanation can be laden with academic vocabulary, from 'classify', 'regulate', 'insulate', 'hypothalamus' and 'homeostasis' in a Biology lesson; to 'flamboyant', 'formative', 'contemporaries', 'pares down' and 'experimental' in a GCSE Art lesson.[17] When children are busy grappling with tricky words that they don't know, it obviously hampers their learning.

The reality is that for any given classroom of children, regardless of our grouping model, children will have issues that hamper their reading. Children will have lots of gaps in their background knowledge and their word knowledge. If we better understand these reading processes, we can better notice when our students are struggling to read, or how we can better challenge and support them to read more difficult texts.

## What do good readers do?

Given the complexity of the act of reading, there are a lot of opportunities for it to go wrong. If any single strand of the 'Big Five' is insecure, then a child can fail to properly comprehend what they read. In the hurly-burly of the classroom, miscomprehensions and gaps in word knowledge and background knowledge can remain hidden. To better help children like James, we had better start with unveiling what a good reader does habitually.

Let me share another portrait of one of my students, Jane, who will also prove recognisable to any teacher. Jane is a successful student. She deploys an array of strategies so automatically, with such confidence and fluency, that it can be hard for anyone to think that reading in this fashion wasn't just '*natural*' for Jane. Sat quietly reading a tricky text, Jane's stillness can belie a whirring mental activity that sees her draw upon her vast store of background knowledge and a wealth of words.

So what are the common factors that mark out good readers like Jane? The following list is an attempt to make visible the expertise of successful readers:

- Good readers decode words fluently, quickly mapping out their meaning, connecting them to their prior background knowledge.
- Good readers possess a broad and deep vocabulary knowledge.
- Good readers actively draw upon their broad background knowledge to make sense of the text.
- Good readers read quickly, accurately and with the appropriate expression.
- Good readers read for longer, with greater effort and persistence.[18]
- Good readers read a lot and are repeatedly exposed to vocabulary, gaining a depth of word knowledge, and they are better served with yet more background knowledge.
- Good readers have a sound knowledge of text structures, seeking out structural conventions like headings to organise their knowledge into memorable patterns.

- Good readers automatically deploy comprehension strategies, like predicting or summarising.
- Good readers constantly monitor their comprehension, asking questions like 'does this make sense?'

Just the act of asking simple questions about what you have read takes a lot of skill and knowledge. Faced with any new topic, from quantum physics to Romantic poetry, Jane asks lots of questions as she reads. Before she reads, she would instinctively ask: What genre is this? Have I read this before? What gaps are there in my knowledge of this topic? As she reads, she would continue to question: Am I getting the main point here? How does this text link to the other reading I have done? What does this word mean in this context? After reading – yes – more questions: Could I summarise or explain this text? What more do I need to know?

Now, as Jane develops as a more mature reader in secondary school, she accumulates an implicit awareness that how she reads in history is quite unique in style. Just a few yards down the school corridor, she then subtly shifts her perspective when she reads in English. In history, faced with sources related to the civil rights movement in the United States, Jane considers the author of the source, their political stance and other cues regarding their credibility. In English literature, Jane would consider the author and their place in history: whether they are part of a literary movement, or whether they follow the traditions of a genre and more. In computer science – well, the perspective of the author becomes relatively unimportant – reading becomes more about following sequences and logic – stripped of any sense of historical meaning. Jane would instead concentrate on the logic of the instructions and the language of the code.

For James, he may have managed with the stories and straightforward texts of his childhood, but they fail to offer him the reading strategies to navigate the different modes of reading as he moves from one academic subject to another. He may even read some great fiction at home, but he still lacks the specialist vocabulary and reading strategies required to flourish when reading in the academic disciplines.

The obvious problem here is the yawning gap between how Jane and James think and act when they read.

Even for the most responsive teachers, we can assume that James would ask basic questions like: What do I know about this topic? What genre is this text? What words do I know in this passage? Sadly, James simply lacks awareness as a reader. All too often, children like James have their thinking clogged up by trying to understand difficult academic words, leaving him with little mental energy to make sense of what he has read, or to repair his miscomprehensions.

There is no quick fix when it comes to accumulating the knowledge and strategies of a good reader. There are no quick fixes when it comes to accumulating something like a 50,000-word vocabulary. Simply allocating more time to silent reading will not be enough.[19] We need to teach and scaffold reading with skill in the classroom, founded upon a better knowledge of how we read successfully, and the barriers to good reading. Only then can we begin to close the achievement gap and help students like James read successfully like Jane.

After reading this chapter, I would challenge every teacher to find out more about reading. This very short summary really is just a starting point – it is imperative that we all confidently understand how children learn to read and go on to read to learn best.

**IN SHORT...**

- We all develop *'mental models'* when we read. Therefore, when reading a story, children develop a picture of characters and settings, drawing upon their prior knowledge of story structures, genres and typical vocabulary choices. The more we read, the better our 'mental models' and the deeper our understanding of what we read in a given topic or subject.

- We have many more sounds than we have letters in the English language, and so it is a complex 'deep orthography' that proves harder to learn than 'shallow' counterparts such as Spanish or Finnish. Learning this alphabetic code in a systematic fashion is crucial in establishing the first building blocks for reading.

- The 'Simple View of Reading' shows how reading is a not-so-simple process of decoding words then unpacking their meaning. The 'reading rope' is a helpful analogy for how we need to develop multiple skills concurrently to read with success. Vocabulary knowledge is an integral strand in the rope.

- The 'Big Five' is a crucial framework for understanding how children learn to read and how we should teach reading. It is a starting point for teachers to better understand how aspects of reading, like fluency, vocabulary and comprehension, relate and interact.

- Poor readers don't do many of the things we expect they do when reading and so they need explicit modelling of successful reading strategies.

# Notes

1 Seidenberg, M. (2017). *Language at the speed of sight: How we read, why so many can't and what can be done about it.* New York, NY: Basic Books, p. 29.
2 McCutchen, D., Harry, D. R., Cox, S., Sidman, S. Covill, E. A., & Cunningham, A. E. (2002). 'Reading teachers' knowledge of children's literature and English phonology'. *Annals of Dyslexia*, 52 (1): 205–228.
3 Connor, C. M., Piasta, S. B., Fishman, B., Glasney, S., Schatschneider, C., Crowe, E., Underwood, P., & Morrison, F. J. (2009). 'Individualizing student instruction precisely: Effects of child x instruction interactions on first graders' literacy development'. *Child Development Journal*, 80 (1): 77–100. doi: 10.1111/j.1467-8624.2008.01247.x.
4 Podhajski, B., Mather, N., Nathan, J., & Sammons, J. (2009). 'Professional development in scientifically based reading instruction: Teacher knowledge and reading outcomes'. *Journal of Learning Disabilities*, 42 (5): 403–417. doi: 10.1177/0022219409338737.
5 Joseph Rowntree Foundation. (2016). '5 million adults lack basic literacy and numeracy skills'. Accessed online on 14 December 2017 at: www.jrf.org.uk/press/5-million-adults-lack-basic-literacy-and-numeracy-skills.
6 Scarborough, H. S. (2001). 'Connecting early language and literacy to later reading (dis)abilities: Evidence, theory, and practice'. In S. Neuman & D. Dickinson (eds.), *Handbook for research in early literacy* (pp. 97–110). New York, NY: Guilford Press.
7 Education Endowment Foundation (2017). *Improving literacy in key stage two: guidance report.* London: Education Endowment Foundation. Accessed online on 14 December 2017 at: http://bit.ly/2xKUKHf.
8 National Reading Panel (US) (2000). Report of the National Reading Panel: Teaching children to read: An evidence-based assessment of the scientific research literature on reading and its implications for reading instruction: Reports of the subgroups. Washington, DC: National Institute of Child Health and Human Development, National Institutes of Health.

9 The size of the English language lexicon is a matter of much debate, with different interpretations, but this is a handy guidepost.

10 Moats, L. (1999). 'Reading is like rocket science: What expert teachers of reading should know and be able to do'. Washington, DC: The American Federation of Teachers. Accessed online on 12 December 2015 at: www.ldaustralia. org/client/documents/Teaching%20Reading%20is%20 Rocket%20Science%20-%20Moats.pdf.

11 Ouellette, G. P. (2006). 'What's meaning got to do with it: The role of vocabulary in word reading and reading comprehension'. *Journal of Educational Psychology*, 98 (3): 554–566.

12 Seidenberg, M. (2017). *Language at the speed of sight: How we read, why so many can't and what can be done about it.* New York, NY: Basic Books, p. 61.

13 National Reading Panel (US) (2000): ibid.

14 Benjamin, A. (2017). *Infusing vocabulary into the reading-writing workshop: A guide for teachers in Grades K–8.* London: Rutledge.

15 Firth, J. R. (1957). *Papers in linguistics.* Oxford: Oxford University Press.

16 Nation, K. (2005). 'Children's reading comprehension difficulties'. In M. J. Snowling and C. Hulme (eds.), *The science of reading: A handbook* (pp. 248–265). Oxford: Blackwell Publishing Ltd. doi: 10.1002/9780470757642.ch14.

17 These terms are drawn from a short video on the Welsh artists Augustus John and Gwen John, filmed for the BBC Bitesize website: BBC Bitesize. Accessed online on 17 July 2017 at: www.bbc.co.uk/education/clips/z7xkjxs.

18 Guthrie, J. T., Wigfield, A., & Klauda, S. L. (2012). 'Adolescents' engagement in academic literacy' (Report No. 7). Accessed online on 15 July 2017 at: www.corilearning.com/research-publications.

19 Baker, L. (2002). 'Metacognition in comprehension instruction'. In C. C. Block & M. Pressley (eds.), *Comprehension instruction: Research-based best practices* (pp. 77–95). New York, NY: Guilford.

# 3 What is in a word? Know your roots

The judicious author's mind is enthralled by etymology.
*Lyrical ballads* preface, 1815, by William Wordsworth

Our knowledge of words is inextricably bound to our knowledge of the world. Words have depth, their own histories and biographies, revealing to us no less than the archaeology of human thought and history. Too often though, our focus on vocabulary in schools is shallow. We share a glossary here, attempt to explain a word there, offer up a quiz question or two. Habitually then, we fail to plumb the rich depths of words that can unlock essential knowledge and understanding.

We began this book with the assertion that a child leaving school with a word-hoard of something like 50,000 words would possess the tools to thrive in school and beyond. Let's compare that with a little snapshot from our nation's history. A good estimate would put the entire lexicon of Old English at around 50,000 words. Our students then, influenced by over 1300 years of history, would outdo any ancient bard. In an age of incessant teenager bashing, let's give them some credit!

The histories of words (**etymology** is the study of the history of words, their origins and how they change over time) are all around us and they prove much more than a mere curiosity. We know that around 60% of our English lexicon is drawn from a combination of Latin and Greek origins,[1] with the more technical vocabulary of school reaching even higher, to something like 90%.[2] When children learn the story and the deeper meaning of a word, it can prove memorable and revelatory. Given the consistent origins of our academic vocabulary, we are surely missing a teaching trick.

There are many Latin loan words that are commonly used in our language and are obviously Latin in origin, such as 'bona fide', 'circa' and 'vice versa'. Less obvious Latin loan words include 'agenda', 'futile' and, ironically, the word 'obvious' (see Appendix 1: A list of common Latin loan words). By making the roots of the English language more obvious, we present many teachable moments.

We can see the challenges of old-fashioned words in many subject areas. The language of science has been described as a "monolithic castle of impenetrable speech".[3] This complex academic language is not easily picked up in general wider reading, but even a rather basic awareness of etymology can help to demystify it. Take the word 'science' itself. It shares the root from the Indo-European 'skein', meaning 'to cut'. You can see it hidden in words like 'scythe' and 'scissors', but also in the word 'science' – as in 'separating out'.[4] Happily, the word 'shit' derives from the same origins of 'science' and the root 'skei', as we unceremoniously cut waste from our body.

Try that little etymological nugget out in your next science lesson!

These stories that attend the words we use – some obscure, others commonly known – can make abstract and complex academic concepts more concrete and clear for children. Take another word commonly used in science: 'dehydrogenate'. When you unpick the word, you find the root 'hydrogen' – from 'hydro', meaning 'water', and 'gen', meaning 'to bring forth'. Then the prefix 'de' is a common one and means 'to remove' as well as 'descent, and lessening intensity', with the suffix 'ate' meaning 'to act'. This big, complex word then tells its own story in its composite parts (**morphology** is the study of word parts: roots, prefixes and suffixes). Here then, hydrogen is being removed from a compound.

Given the vast majority of our scientific lexicon is derived from pretty reliable and stable etymological roots and word parts, we can use this as a tool for teaching reading and scientific knowledge with precise understanding. It sparks a curiosity and pursuit of knowledge and reason that is so apt for the science classroom.

Every word we use in school has a story and a history. Many academic words have their meaning encoded into their spellings, with some unique anomalies and grammatical variations. We have 'geese' and not 'gooses', but if you travel to the United States, do you encounter 'mooses' and not 'meese'? Whereas 'moose' is a relatively new American word, by contrast, 'goose' has ancient Germanic etymology (it shares the same plural variation of 'tooth' and 'teeth'). These different word biographies account for their different meanings and spellings.

The stark reality is that most teachers are uncomfortable, or simply not familiar, with tackling vocabulary beyond sharing dictionary definitions and using the context of the sentence to teach a word.[5,6] We may teach words like 'democracy', 'plutocracy', 'oligarchy' and 'monarchy' in history, citizenship and politics, but do we help students make meaningful, rich connections between those words? The information is readily at hand. The suffix 'cracy' means 'power', with 'archy' meaning 'rulership'; 'demo' means 'people', with 'pluto' meaning 'wealth'; 'oligo' meaning 'few' and 'mono' meaning 'one/alone'. By foregrounding the word parts and the stories underpinning them, we unlock their meaning.

As the eminent psychologist Dan Willingham stated, "Stories are psychologically privileged in the human heart". When our explanations of difficult academic concepts and ideas are clothed with the stories of our rich linguistic history, we offer our students a deeper understanding of the complex academic language of school. When students begin, either consciously or subconsciously, to make connections between words, to see word parts and roots emerging within words as they listen or read, they begin to unlock a powerful armoury of tools for reading independently. Armed with these tools, children become 'word detectives', uncovering layers of meaning in language that prove revealing, intriguing and liberating.

My experience as a teacher is that children love finding out about the world within a word. It proves fun, challenging and for many children, it can unleash a love of learning.

## More than just 50,000 words: The importance of 'word depth'

Size matters. A word-hoard of something like 50,000 to 60,000 words is a good proxy for what vocabulary children need to leave school with in order to thrive academically and beyond. Of course, it isn't all about size. 'Word depth' is integral for understanding what we read and communicating with success in academic contexts and more. How well you know such words is likely more important than how many you know. As you would expect though, there is a reciprocal relationship between the size of our vocabulary and the depth and degree to which we understand those words.

When words like 'root' appear in a text, readers make quick judgments, mapping which meaning of the word 'root' is most appropriate to the meaning and context of the sentence and the text. In this chapter, the noun relating to the origins of words is most likely, whereas in more common usage, the meaning usually relates to the 'root' of a plant. This intuitive search for meaning that connects that word 'root' to our background knowledge and our related known words is typically an unconscious process, occurring constantly, as we talk or read, within or outside of the classroom. Too often though, these processes remain hidden as we talk and read, so miscomprehensions and gaps in word knowledge go unchecked.

A well-established concept from linguistic research that is helpful is the '**lexical quality hypothesis**'[7] ('lexis' simply proving the fancy linguistic term for vocabulary). This describes how well a child knows a word, the 'quality' of your word knowledge. When a child has a multifaceted knowledge of a word, such as the pronunciation of the word, its spelling, any multiple meanings, common categories, word families and so on, then the better the 'quality'.

By way of example of the '*lexical quality hypothesis*', the more exposure a child has to a given word, such as 'tectonic' in geography, the more deeply the word becomes known to them. The etymology of the word, from the Greek 'tectonicus', meaning 'related to building', is slightly different to the geology specific meaning relating to the structure of the earth's crust. Deeply understanding this word requires more than etymological knowledge, or simply spelling the word with accuracy. It has related words and concepts from geology, like 'tectonic plates' and 'tectonic hazards', which children need to know. Word knowledge helps connect together ideas and concepts. Without this degree of 'word depth' then, understanding important geographical phenomena like the theory of 'Continental drift' becomes impossible.

As an English teacher, I reteach the meaning (and often the spelling) of 'metaphor' as a frustrating annual ritual. Every year seemingly, students forget the meaning and spelling of this important literary term. It is a regular reminder of the crucial importance of students possessing 'word depth'.

We should stop and ask ourselves: how often do we pay explicit attention to the 'word depth' of the vocabulary we teach and use?

The quick accommodation of new words into our word-hoard can occur with just a single exposure to that word. In music, the word 'dynamics', meaning 'the level of sound, for example, loud or soft, in a piece of music', has a singular meaning that can be successfully assimilated into the general knowledge of young musicians. More commonly, however, learning academic words is a slower, cumulative process with most complex academic words requiring multiple exposures to achieve 'word depth'. The research indicates anything between four and ten exposures for a new word can best establish a word long-term memory so that it can be deeply understood and used by students.[8] Using a word four times or more has obvious ramifications for teaching a curriculum.

Given teachers are often pushed for time, allocating much time for explicit, repeated instruction of vocabulary would likely prove a difficult proposition. And yet, if we can make such explanations of words concise and precise in our classroom talk, explaining the etymology and morphology where appropriate, then we are talking about small margins of time that offer a depth of understanding that can be critical to children's learning. Quite frankly, we need to make time for teaching vocabulary.

Merely decorating a child's schoolbook with a subject specific glossary is not enough. A planned approach to explaining words, including meaningful repeated exposures to those words, will help our children to confidently develop 'word depth'. As teachers then, we need to be more conscious of the language we use in our daily classroom talk. Too easily, we can use metaphors and idioms, like 'she was on a real high' or 'he was green with envy', that are a wholly natural part of our speech, but can actually obscure meaning for children (remember the obstacle here for EAL children in particular).

Teachers, like children, develop when we pay careful attention to the words we communicate and teach '**word consciousness**'. When you understand the importance of 'word depth', it can fundamentally change your way of thinking and teaching, and you become '*word conscious*'. We become curious in the pursuit of understanding the language we had largely taken for granted. When children develop 'word consciousness', it initiates a new way of thinking that can prove of life-long worth for our students.

As teachers cannot elaborate on the rich etymological biographies of *every* word (unless they have previously learned Latin and/or Greek – alas, I have not), we need to ensure that we better select words to explain more comprehensively. Alongside selecting words to teach, we can help our students to develop '*word consciousness*' themselves. The simple notion of teaching etymology or morphology more deliberately doesn't just teach a handful of important subject specific words; it opens up a different way of reading and even thinking for our students.

For bilingual students, we draw upon their advantage of linking **cognates** – words with common etymological origins across different languages, for example, the German cognate for 'friend' is 'freund' – as we teach. Indeed, when teaching modern foreign languages, as well as ancient languages, drawing upon knowledge of etymology and morphology is an integral aspect of teaching. When such learning becomes the habitual norm of every classroom, we give our children the means to better use and understand the academic language of school.

Let's try this theory out.

Take the prefix 'nom', from the Latin *nominalis* 'pertaining to a name or names', from *'nomen'*, meaning 'name'. Words like 'nominate', 'nominee', 'nomenclature', 'ignomy' and 'binomial' all begin to make sense as words that have their roots related to the concept of naming. When faced with the word 'nominal', children can draw upon their background knowledge and morphological knowledge and understanding. They have a memorable hook. When they study French, they recognise that 'nom' means 'name'.

Now, consider an important word that you teach commonly. What is its word family? Are there recognisable word parts? Is the word history particularly revealing? When we begin to do this with a cluster of important words we teach, we begin to unveil a new, useful layer of knowledge for our explanations, as well as more memorable hooks for the ideas and concepts that we teach.

In maths, practice of equations can be undertaken with little need for lengthy forays into language; however, teacher explanations, and student understanding, can be enriched by quickly making explicit the Latin and Greek morphemes that make up the mathematical lexicon. Take 'tri', denoting 'three', or 'poly', meaning 'many'. When students recognise the root of 'poly' being many, then many more words become easier to decipher: 'polygon', 'polynomial', 'polymath', 'polymer' and so on (just be wary of a debate on polygamy!). Given the frequency of these words, we can easily recognise the usefulness of explicit instruction of such prefixes.

This type of *'word conscious'* instruction happens in classrooms every day, but all too often, it is haphazard or unplanned. Children fail to see the consistent patterns and common meanings found in academic vocabulary. Too much of the academic language of school remains implicit. Those children who are word rich rapidly grow their vocabulary regardless, but those children with small word-hoards are disadvantaged by missed opportunities.

## Etymology for every teacher

Etymology – the study of the origin of words and the way in which their meanings have changed throughout history.

The fascinating origins of the English language are all around us, woven intricately into the fabric of our lives and stamped indelibly into our daily talk.

The Latinate structure of our language is all around us, but often it is invisible even to the most educated amongst us. Take 'AM' and 'PM'. How many people could actually name the Latin words for these abbreviations? The answer is 'ante meridiem', meaning 'before midday', and 'post meridiem', denoting 'after midday'. Perhaps we make the common mistake of 'RIP' denoting 'rest in peace', rather than the original 'requiescat in pace'? Now, you could fairly argue that such knowledge is largely redundant, but then we close down rich opportunities to broaden the vocabulary of our children and we choose to hide the primary roots of our academic communication.

The most common words in the English language are trusty Anglo-Saxon stalwarts like 'and', 'but', 'by', 'have', 'with' and so on, but the Norman Invasion of 1066 didn't just bring us sturdy castles and the feudal system. The Normans ushered in an epoch-making shift in the English language. The French people who settled in England first changed the language of the law and the professions. Our modern academic language is subsequently indebted to the influences of Latin and Greek, and latterly French – termed rather nicely as the 'Romance languages'.

For a millennium, Latin learning has been synonymous with being educated. Still, it hasn't stopped some detractors who labelled Latinate words derogatorily as 'ink horn words' – linked to the small vessel holding ink, showing how these long words wasted ink. Using over-elaborate language has received criticism ever since. George Orwell famously scorned Latin words that "falls upon the facts like soft snow, blurring the outlines and covering up all the details" in his *Politics and the English language*. Of course, when he criticised such "pretentious diction" he would have been better placed if both 'pretentious' and 'diction' did not have French and Latin origins.

We can see the shift from relatively short Saxon words to longer Latinate vocabulary in everyday words in the following table.[9]

| Anglo-Saxon origin | Latin and Greek origins |
| --- | --- |
| 'Ask' | 'Interrogate' |
| 'Begin' | 'Commence' |
| 'Belly' | 'Abdomen' |
| 'Deer' | 'Venison' |
| 'Fire' | 'Conflagration' |
| 'Horse' | 'Equestrian' |
| 'Loving' | 'Amorous' |
| 'Nightly' | 'Nocturnal' |

You can see the pattern that emerges. Words of Latin and Greek origin are not just longer, though that is a clear consequence of the influence of more prefixes and suffixes, but they are more precise. For academic subjects, such precision matters.

Now, Orwell did have a point: we wouldn't expect anybody to go around speaking with an elaborate Latinate diction as they order milk at the shop, but it is equally clear that the sophisticated language of school correlates strongly with the Latin and Greek origins of the English language. Teaching with etymology in mind is therefore a reliable and helpful tool, not just for English teachers, but also for every classroom teacher. In fact, it may prove more valuable for teachers of maths, science and geography, given the narrower roots of their subject specific language.

You could rightly ask, why aren't ancient languages like Latin on the curriculum for all? Why do we still perceive the powerful roots of our language as exclusive to the few who already prove word rich? Here, we could also speculate about how useful it would prove for English teachers to learn an ancient language as part of their professional development and enrichment.

Children are curious pattern seekers and makers. If they are only taught the complexities of language penned within in the straightjacket of word lists, they will miss out on a wealth of intriguing knowledge. A problem here is that studying language and grammar typically has little glamour. But remember Willingham's statement about stories being "psychologically privileged"? The potentially dry, lifeless learning attached to word lists and grammar drills can be transformed by the power of stories.

By way of example, did you know that 'grammar' and 'glamour' actually share a family history? 'Grammar', back in the fourteenth century had a variant 'gramary', meaning 'learning and erudition', which was aligned with 'magic and enchantment'. 'Glamour' is a Scottish variation of 'grammar' – later taking on the sense of a 'magical beauty and charm'. So a witch would 'cast a glamour' – an illusion or spell. The next time a child bemoans practising grammar, you can regale them with a tale of the glamorous Scots and their interest in the occult!

Take the word *'symbiosis'* from biology. It means 'union for life of two different organisms based on mutual benefit'. Deriving from the Greek, meaning simply 'living together', you can break the word down further. 'Bio', as we know famously means *'life'* – hence 'biology' – with the prefix *'sym'*, which is an altered version of the Greek 'syn' meaning, 'with, together with, along with, in the company of'. Think of *'symmetry'* – when things go along together in proportion, or 'sympathy', when your emotions become enmeshed together with another. Symbiosis can benefit from being linked to 'sympathy' in our student's minds. Such stories, connections and patterns are everywhere in our language.

The value of a child having this deep etymological knowledge of 'symbiosis' is quickly multiplied, as the word is usable in a variety of academic contexts, such as an analysis of characters in a novel in English literature, to describing environments in geography. Though some words no doubt have disputed etymological roots, even debating this itself generates meaningful knowledge of our language and our world.

Of course, word knowledge begets more word knowledge. When a child knows the root 'tract' in 'sub<u>tract</u>ion' in mathematics, they can recognise the common root in other words, like 'de<u>tract</u>', 'in<u>tract</u>able', 'ex<u>tract</u>', 'dis<u>tract</u>', 'a<u>ttrac</u><u>tion</u>' and even '<u>tractor</u>'. Meaningful patterns abound. We need only make these implicit linguistic patterns explicit. As the root 'tract' means 'to drag or to pull', perhaps the next time we hear about someone being "on the pull" we can debate the etymological relationship between 'attraction' and 'tractor' … or maybe not!

How then do we mobilise etymological knowledge for a range of teachers each with different degrees of linguistic knowledge?

A quick foray on the Internet can prove fruitful and a search of key terms around 'etymology', 'vocabulary' and related search terms quickly generates useful resources:

- The go-to **etymology search** website for your word search needs is www.etymonline.com.
- **Latin and Greek word root lists** are easily available, such as here: http://bit.ly/1LkliAU.
- An excellent **Latin dictionary** can be found here: www. perseus.tufts.edu/hopper/ or here: http://latindictionary. wikidot.com/start.
- '**Membean**' offers some excellent word root tree-diagrams that are handy for teaching: http://membean. com/wordroots.
- '**Vocabulary.com**' has a superb array of word root and prefix lists, with examples, definitions and activities, which can be found here: www.vocabulary.com/lists/ morphology-and-roots/.

Such searches are quick and easy. When we select important words in our lesson planning, or long-term planning, we can supplement them by using these teaching resources. A key action should be collaborative planning within and across schools, to identify the words to teach explicitly and to decide upon the essential etymological knowledge to share in a structured way with students. Many hands make light work in this regard.

Another fascinating support factor for teachers looking to share etymological knowledge is the emergence of programmes like *'Classics in Communities'*, launched back in 2013, and the national charity *'Classics for All'* (www. classicsforall.org.uk), that works with over 100 schools to promote the learning of the classics.

Here, Dr Arlene Holmes-Henderson, from the University of Oxford, is working to change the perception of studying the classics:

For too long, Latin has been seen as the preserve of the 'most able' – students who were selected to participate in 'gifted and talented' programmes. My research shows that the impact on literacy for these students is minimal, as their knowledge and skills are already advanced. The impact for students with low levels of literacy, however, can be transformative.

Dr Arlene Holmes-Henderson, personal communication, 10 April 2017

Pervasive and deep-seated misconceptions about the appropriate curriculum for word rich children, compared to those who do not possess a broad academic vocabulary, serve to perpetuate the vocabulary gap. Holmes-Henderson relates the value of every child experiencing classical languages like Greek and Latin with the "crucial benefit that children can more deeply understand what words mean". Though it no doubt helps to have expert support, or perhaps to have studied a course in the classics, you don't *need* to have studied the classics to teach vocabulary expertly in the classroom.[10]

Students can be encouraged to create their own '**root word trees**' or word histories, rather than simply passively taking possession of a Latin and Greek word list. Discussion, research, homework and so on, can all be infused with vocabulary learning. They begin to recognise that each subject discipline has unique language with shared roots in history, making it less alien to them – helping to close the word gap between their personal language and the academic language of school. In subjects like drama, science, politics, maths and geography, the Greek origins of discipline become obvious. In uncovering the history of language like this, we foster the natural curiosity of children and open up a rich, complex world of valuable knowledge.

## The power of morphology

Morphology – the study of parts of things, and in linguistics, the study of word parts, for example, roots, prefixes and suffixes.

When we take simple everyday vocabulary, like 'work' or 'employ', we recognise the flexibility of these words to grow, change and become more elaborate and precise. With additional **prefixes** at the beginnings of words and **suffixes** at the ends of words, 'work' can become 're-work-ing', 'employ' can become 'un-employ-able' or 'un-employ-ment'. It is this foundational knowledge of language that sees the vocabulary of children rapidly grow in the early school years. Knowledge of individual words grows exponentially as children develop knowledge of word families, prefixes and suffixes.

Each word comes with its word family, from simple **inflections** (the name given to the extra letter or letters to a noun, adjective or verb, for example, 'happy' becomes 'happier', 'trip' becomes 'trips'), to words that change meaning by adding familiar prefixes, such as 'fit' becoming 'unfit'. This has obvious implications for expanding children's vocabularies.

Examples abound. In fact, let's take the word 'bound'. It is a **polysemous** word – that is to say, a word that has multiple meanings. These words typically prove a particularly common barrier for children with a narrow vocabulary. 'Bound' can mean a leap; being set for a destination; being tied by rope; and so on. Inflections include 'abound', 'bounds', 'unbound', 'bounding', 'rebound' and 'boundary'. We then add **compound words** – a combination of two or more words – like 'spellbound', 'duty-bound' and 'desk-bound'. Now, some of these variations can trip up children, as their meaning shifts, but the principle that learning one single word invariably opens up a family of related words is sound.

Children can and will recognise word families implicitly, mapping new words onto familiar words, spying inflections, instinctively hearing familiar sounds in words (remember phonemic awareness from Chapter 2?). We can go one better and properly coordinate this growing knowledge and understanding of words and word families. A great deal of research evidence shows that teaching children to analyse the morphology of words helps them to learn the meaning of new words.[11,12,13] Simply, with little tweaks to our practice, like asking children about what words bound might be related to, or sound like, can open up a powerful dialogue.

By way of example, in English, I could quickly and simply flag up the word root 'log' (from Greek 'logos'), meaning 'word' – with 'ology' meaning 'study of' (familiar of course from the many subjects in the school timetable). When you offer a sample of words that contain the root in English, like 'dialogue', 'monologue', 'prologue', 'epilogue', 'chronological', 'eulogy', 'neologism', 'analogous', 'anthology', 'syllogism' and much more, you open up a wealth of connections. With consistent practice, children become '**word detectives**', seeking out patterns, making links and finding meaning.

As the academic language of school has so many Latin and Greek roots – particularly subject domains like maths, the sciences and much more, we can devote time to identifying common word parts. Many words, particularly those from the scientific domains, have morphemes that consistently reveal the very specific meaning of the word. For example, the prefix 'ex-' or 'exo-' (from Latin) is very common in science, meaning 'out of/away from/external or outside' – most commonly recognised in the word 'external'. We can search out examples in just a sample of scientific words, including the following:

| Scientific term | Definition |
| --- | --- |
| *Exfoliation* | The removal or shedding of cells or scales from the outer tissue surface. |
| *Exocarp* | The botanical term for the outermost layer of the walls of a ripened fruit. |
| *Exogenous* | Growing or originating from outside of an organism. |
| *Exophthalmos* | The abnormal outward bulging of the eyeball. |
| *Exoskeleton* | The hard outer structure that provides support or protection for an organism. |
| *Exothermic* | A chemical reaction that releases heat. |

An analysis of morphology is clearly a useful teaching aid if a chemistry teacher is explaining the difference between 'exothermic' (release energy outwards) and 'endothermic' (take energy in) reactions. Whilst it may not be viable or practical to do a morphological analysis of each and every word we teach, 'word conscious' teachers, and students too, can habitually begin to recognise common word parts.

Every teacher and child should be conscious that an analysis of word parts can sometimes prove misleading. When faced with a common word like 'manslaughter', our common knowledge may quickly consider the crime and the combination of 'man' and 'slaughter', but it is easy for a child lacking background knowledge to misinterpret it as 'mans' 'laughter' combined. We can dig out words within words that lead children to make errors. A simple word like 'cartoon' may appear to be related to the roots of the word 'car', but the root is derived from 'card', not 'car'. Still, even these linguistic dead-ends can prove valuable explorations of a child's knowledge, or their lack thereof, as teachers can help children learn from their mistakes.

For a teacher looking to begin using morphological analysis, to deepen their explanations and to explore the meaningful biography of valuable words in their subject, beginning with common Latin and Greek roots is a sensible place to start. Here is just a small sample of common word roots that could be used with students to prompt their 'word consciousness', getting them to seek out their own examples:

| Root | Original language | English examples |
|------|-------------------|------------------|
| *Aud* (to hear) | Latin | Audible, auditory |
| *Bio* (life) | Greek | Biology, biography, biosphere |
| *Dic/dict* (to speak or say) | Latin | Predict, dictate, contradict |
| *Fract* (to break) | Latin | Fracture, fragment, fractal |
| *Geo* (earth) | Greek | Geography, geology, geothermal |
| *Graph/gram* (to write or draw) | Greek | Graphic, graphology, grammar |
| *Micro/mini* (small) | Greek/Latin | Microscope, microbe, minority |
| *Phon* (sound) | Greek | Microphone, cacophony, phone |
| *Photo* (light) | Greek | Photograph, photon, phonology |
| *Port* (to carry) | Latin | Export, transport, portfolio |
| *Rupt* (to break) | Latin | Rupture, eruption, interruption |
| *Scop* (to see or watch) | Greek | Scope, horoscope, microscopic |
| *Spec/spect* (to look at) | Latin | Spectator, speculate, spectrum |
| *Struct* (to build) | Latin | Construction, construe, instructor |

| *Tele (far)* | Greek | Telephone, telescope, television |
| *Tract (to pull or draw)* | Latin | Detract, subtract, attraction |
| *Vis/vid (to see or look)* | Latin | Vision, video, advisory |

Many of these roots offer up perfect insights into the meaning of words we use daily. Take the 'dict' root and examine the word 'verdict'. 'Ver', meaning 'truth', combined with 'dict', meaning 'to speak' clearly explains the word. 'Veracity' and 'verisimilitude' are part of the same family.

We can help children to understand the complex relationships between words by looking into their roots and chunking word parts. We can help students connect up the Greek and Latin roots used to describe the human body, such as 'caput', 'ora'/'os', 'dens', 'gaster', 'neuron', 'manus', 'ped'/'podos', 'derma', carnem', 'oss', 'cor'/'cardia' and 'psyche'. We can create other memorable categories, such as people and how they organise into groups, such as 'anthropos', 'civis', 'demos', 'ethnos', 'genus', 'populus' and 'socius' (see Appendix 2 for Latin roots related to the human body, people and groups). Creating memorable categories in this fashion can prove an effective word building strategy that makes vocabulary development organised and explicit.

Prefixes and suffixes have played an essential role in the growth of the English language, with around 100 of them being present in around half of the words in our language.[14] Prefixes are particularly useful to teach because there are relatively few of them. Some 20 prefixes comprise around 97% of prefixed words,[15] with four prefixes – 'un', 're', 'in' and 'dis' – accounting for well over half of all prefixed words. There are some common false prefixes, like 'uncle' (it comes from the Latin 'avunculus', meaning 'mother's brother'), but these are few and far between.

Again, prefixes and etymology combine usefully and meaningfully. 'Dis', meaning 'apart, away' has negative connotations. In the word 'discord', we combine 'dis' with 'cord', Latin for 'heart'. The word then metaphorically represents our heart and mind being separated from another. The common prefixes 'pre', meaning 'before', and 'post', meaning 'after', are not usually combined together, but they are in the word 'preposterous'. 'Pre' comes before 'post' meaning literally 'before after', a confusing and topsy-turvy state of affairs.

Once more, we can begin to meaningfully group prefixes into clusters that foreground patterns in our language:

- Prefixes denoting negation: **'dis'**, **'un'**, **'im'**, **'ir'** and **'non'**.
- Prefixes denoting position: **'pre'**, **'fore'**, **'mid'**, **'into'** and **'post'**.
- Prefixes denoting over/under position: **'super'**, **'over'** and **'sub'**.
- Prefixes denoting togetherness: **'com'**, **'con'** and **'co'**.
- Prefixes denoting negative qualities: **'mal'** and **'mis'**.
- Prefixes denoting being against something or someone: **'anti'** and **'contra'**.
- Prefixes denoting number: **'uni'**, **'mono'**, **'bi'**, **'tri'**, **'quad'**, **'penta'**, **'dec'**, **'cent'**, **'sex'**, **'hex'**, **'sept'**, **'octo'**, **'non'** and **'semi'**.
- Other useful prefixes: **'re'**, **'trans'**, **'de'**, **'ex'** and **'under'**.

We can start with the most common prefixes and go from there, as shown in the following table:

| Prefix | Meaning | Example |
|---|---|---|
| **Anti-** | Against | Antibody |
| **De-** | Down, down from, off | Decline |
| **Dis-** | Not, opposite of | Disembodied |

| En-, Em- | To cause | Enable |
|---|---|---|
| Fore- | Before | Foreground |
| In-, im- | In | Insidious |
| In-, im-, il-, ir- | Not | Illegal, irreligious |
| Inter- | Between | Interregnum |
| Mal- | Bad | Malformed |
| Mid- | Middle | Midnight |
| Mis- | Wrong | Misinformed |
| Non- | Not | Non-payment |
| Over- | Over | Overwrought |
| Pre- | Before | Precondition |
| Post- | After | Postgraduate |
| Re- | Again | Reassert |
| Semi- | Half | Semiaquatic |
| Sub- | Under | Submarine |
| Super- | Above | Superannuation |
| Trans- | Across | Transverse |
| Un- | Not | Unassuming |
| Under- | Under | Underwhelming |

There are many opportunities to foster and consolidate knowledge of prefixes and their key part in vocabulary building with explicit teaching. Once we identify prefixes we can follow some simple steps as proposed by Graves and Hammond:[16]

1 Present the prefix in isolation and also attached to four words (e.g. 'Dis': 'disability', 'disagree', 'disbelief' and 'disown').
2 Define the prefix (e.g. dis – meaning 'apart, away').
3 Use the whole words in sentences (e.g. 'The children stared in disbelief').
4 Define the words (e.g. disbelief – inability or refusal to accept something is true or real; lack of faith).

5 After completing and discussing the above steps, give students an opportunity to find other words exemplifying the prefix.

6 Have students add examples to a vocabulary notebook (or a similar record in their class books).

With some forward planning, we can of course apply this method to teaching an array of word roots. Learning Latin or Greek has a reputation for dour learning-by-rote traditionalism, but this lazy view doesn't fairly characterise the creative pleasure you can foster by exploring word parts and their meanings.

With a little support and imagination, children can be recognising patterns in everything they read, from academic textbooks to comic books. From connecting words within subjects, to coining wholly new words, the limits are endless. Such knowledge of language becomes a new way of thinking and powerful knowledge indeed. Unfamiliar words can become familiar; new words connect to old, with vocabulary and understanding developing in tandem.

We need to dispel the myth that the study of etymology and morphology is only the preserve of the English language or modern foreign language teacher. We need to dispel the myth that the Latin and Greek roots of our language are only for nice, but intermittent enrichment activities for a select few privileged children. Our approach to the roots of language can be systematic and developed through our school curriculum. In so doing, we could address many related issues, like spelling problems (more on this in Chapter 6), whilst developing a broad and deep vocabulary that gives children the tools to access a challenging academic curriculum.

It is clear that looking to the language of our past helps us to best prepare our children for the future.

# IN SHORT…

- When it comes to vocabulary knowledge and school success, 'word depth' is probably more important than the breadth of our vocabulary.

- Over 90% of the vocabulary of academic texts in school has Latin and Greek origins and therefore teaching etymology has positive implications for learning and cracking the academic code of school.

- We can encourage 'word consciousness' in our classrooms, fostering a curiosity and interest in words that sparks deep, rich learning.

- The study of morphology – word parts – is a proven method to enhance reading comprehension (even when learning additional languages). We can better understand academic vocabulary by recognising their common word parts, beginning with word roots then moving onto prefixes.

- There are around 100 prefixes, but they are present in over half of the words in the English language (even more in the texts children read at school). We can focus on high frequency prefixes like 'un', 're', 'in' and 'dis', teaching them explicitly and helping children recognise common patterns and word families.

- Morphology and etymology should not prove an 'enrichment' bolt-on for a select few, but instead an integral aspect of how we communicate the academic language of school to make it understood, giving children the requisite tools to grow their vocabulary.

# Notes

1  Nagy, W., & Anderson, R. (1984). 'The number of words in printed school English'. *Reading Research Quarterly*, 19: 304–330.
2  Green, T. M. (2008). *The Greek and Latin roots of English* (4th ed.). Lanham, MD: Rowman & Littlefield.
3  Montgomery, S. L. (1996). *The scientific voice*. New York, NY: Guilford Press.
4  The roots of the word science are up for debate. See this definition from the online etymology tool (a great resource I use regularly). Accessed online on 14 December 2017 at: www.etymonline.com/index.php?allowed_in_frame=0&search=science.
5  Berne, J. I., & Blachowich, C. L. Z. (2008). 'What reading teachers say about vocabulary instruction: Voices from the classroom'. *The Reading Teacher*, 62 (4): 314–323.
6  Rasinski, T., Samuels, S. J., Hiebert, E., Petscher, Y., & Feller, K. (2011). 'The relationship between a silent reading fluency instructional protocol on students' reading comprehension and achievement in an urban school setting'. *Reading Psychology*, 32 (1): 75–97.
7  Perfetti, C. A., & Hart, L. (2002). 'The lexical quality hypothesis'. In L. Verhoeven (ed.), *Precursors of functional literacy* (pp. 189–213). Philadelphia, PA: John Benjamins.
8  Beck, I., McKeown, M., & Kucan, L. (2002). *Bringing words to life*. New York, NY: Guilford, p. 83.
9  Nagy, W., & Townsend, D. (2012). 'Words as tools: Learning academic vocabulary as language acquisition'. *Reading Research Quarterly*, 47 (1): 91–108. doi:10.1002/RRQ.011.
10  Holmes-Henderson, A. (2016). 'Teaching Latin and Greek in primary classrooms: The Classics in Communities project'. *Journal of Classics Teaching*, 17 (33): 50–53.
11  Nagy, W., Berninger V. W., & Abbott R. D. (2006). 'Contributions of morphology beyond phonology to literacy outcomes of upper elementary and middle-school students'. *Journal of Educational Psychology*, 98: 134–147.
12  Carlisle, J. F. (2010). 'Effects of instruction in morphological awareness on literacy achievement: An integrative review'. *Reading Research Quarterly*, 45: 464–487. doi:10.1598/RRQ. 45.4.5.

13  Reed, D. K. (2008). 'A synthesis of morphology interventions and effects on reading outcomes for students in grades K–12'. *Learning Disabilities Research & Practice*, 23: 36–49. doi:10.1111/j.1540-5826.2007.00261.x.

14  Crystal, D. (2012). *The story of English in 100 words*. London: Profile Books.

15  White, T. G., Sowell, J., & Yanagihara, A. (1989). 'Teaching elementary students to use word part clues'. *The Reading Teacher*, 42: 302–308.

16  Graves, M., & Hammond, H. K. (1980). 'A validated procedure for teaching prefixes and its effect on students' ability to assign meanings to novel words'. In M. Kamil and A. Moe (eds.), *Perspectives on reading research and instruction* (pp.184–188). Washington, DC: National Reading Conference.

# 4  Wot d'ya mean by academic vocabulary?

Begin your Bitmap image task by searching in your data representation folder. Then use the hex to denary conversion sheet provided. This is a quick task – just to check if you remember how to manipulate the binary inputs to create an image. I'll take the register whilst you get that completed.

If you want to understand the challenges faced by children grappling with understanding the challenges of academic vocabulary, then I suggest you follow a child through school just for a day. A few months ago, I did just that. I followed a year 10 student, David, during a typical school day at my school. I followed David dutifully as he lugged his over-sized bag from computer science GCSE, to chemistry, German, maths and finally to English literature.

What struck me most following David, as he confidently navigated his well-trodden school timetable, was the strange feeling of being in school, but feeling like a novice again. The calm, expert opening to Mr Brown's computer science lesson – referencing "Bitmap" and "data representation", "hex", "denery" and "manipulate" – immediately submerged me in the complexities of a computer science vocabulary that was alien to me. After just a few minutes, it wasn't just the plastic chairs that made me uncomfortable, but the feeling of being an outsider in a familiar classroom.

Students like David skilfully negotiate their path through the school day. With a broad academic vocabulary, he would go from computer science and onto chemistry, facing its lengthy word equations to exemplify neutralisation, then onto German, with its vast array of new German words, before moving onto mathematics, with its unique combination of words, symbols, numbers, equations and graphs.

What was evident was that David had heard and read academic terms like 'hexadecimal' and 'hydrochloric acid' repeatedly, accumulating 'word depth', connecting them up to related words drawn from his rapidly growing word-hoard. He deftly understood how the term 'variable' had different meanings in computer science, science and maths, and so he could hear and use the word with understanding and apparent ease.

David represents those many privileged children (not necessarily in material terms) who have cracked the academic code of school. David would deftly shift his language from his everyday chat with his friends to then listening and using the academic code that determined success in the classroom. It was hard not to imagine his bag stuffed full of books encompassing a wealth of words – 50,000 or more. David's bag, laden with books, would be carried through that school day, but it will take him to places far beyond school. He will no doubt flourish in school and his wealth of words will offer him the opportunity of making valuable life choices.

Following a student like David through a single school day felt to me like experiencing five different languages. To the many students who don't possess a wealth of words like David, the seemingly secretive code of each classroom can make them feel separate. How many such students are left to mask their failures and insecurities?

75

In such circumstances, occurring in classrooms and schools everywhere, the vocabulary gap can define children's voices and ultimately their life choices.

## Cracking the academic code

Bletchley Park sits opposite the inconspicuous Bletchley train station. A mish-mash of Gothic, Tudor and Baroque architecture, this not-so-grand mansion, hidden away in Milton Keynes, proved to be one of the most crucial settings of the entire Second World War.

The British War Office had attracted women and men: professors, chess champions and the world's best solvers of crossword puzzles to Bletchley Park. Their "peculiar type of work"[1] was code breaking. Housed in shabby huts and blocks, countless 'Spy School' operatives who were sworn to secrecy busily decrypted German army messages across the world, after breaking the crucial 'Enigma code' of the Nazi forces.

The role of unassuming crossword puzzle solvers as pivotal heroes in the most destructive war the world has ever seen, hidden away in huts in Milton Keynes, is a brilliant British story. Fittingly, after the war, Bletchley Park became a teacher training college. Today, as teachers, it is our role to help children in our care to become code breakers of a different sort, but an important one nonetheless.

Words have power. How is it that some children exhibit a confidence in debate with seeming ease? They adapt their language so readily, appearing knowledgeable and authoritative beyond their years. And, yes, they appear powerful. Many such children go onto university interviews, or debating in law chambers, boardrooms, perhaps even parliament, with the same apparent ease.

Children like David exhibit an increasing power in their every communication at school; however, the fact that it is apparently so '*natural*' is deceiving. There is no natural 'gift' here as intimated by the outmoded title of '*gifted and talented*'. The confident speaker is almost always a competent speaker. Their broad and deep vocabulary is the bricks and mortar from which they talk and build their powerful arguments.

The near-hidden process of taking on the academic code of school, and other powerful settings in our wider society, is exposed most strikingly when we see children struggle without it. Quickly, they become marked as the students who simply aren't academic. Children who go on to think that school is simply not for them have absorbed these damaging negative judgments in countless communications in school. For EAL students, we see evidence that taking on a second language can take around four to seven years.[2] Though it can take just under a year for a new speaker of English to be proficient in everyday conversation, acquiring the academic code of school can take seven or more years.[3]

The differences between everyday talk and the complexity of academic talk then are stark and our obligation to teach academic vocabulary is obvious.

Back in 2011, before his sacking as England manager, the Italian, Fabio Capello, described how he used relatively few words with the England football team, "If I need to speak about the economy or other things, I can't, but when you speak about tactics, you don't use a lot of words. I don't have to speak about a lot of different things. Maximum 100 words".[4] Of course, Capello had more than 100 words of English (the typical vocabulary of a 2-year-old), but he reveals a truth that in daily conversation, we use little over the 100 most common words and word families most of the time.

Back in the 1970s, sociologist Basil Bernstein described the difference between a '**restricted code**' and an 'elaborated code'. His idea of the 'restricted code' matches something like that of our typical daily talk. It is spontaneous and informal, full of pauses ('fillers' like 'er' and 'ah'), repetitions, slips and revisions. It is communicated with our body language and references to the world around us. Such language is less dense and of course easier to understand. The 'elaborated code', by contrast, is the academic code of school, university and the professions. It is elaborate and composed of many more rare and complex words.

The difference can be seen in this short example of hypothetical classroom talk:

Everyday talk: It hadn't rained for months. The farmers used new ways of watering the crops to deal with the lack of rain.

Academic talk: Hydration technology was utilised to ease drought.[5]

Clearly, 'how we say it' differs from 'how a scientist says it'. It doesn't mean we have to 'talk like a book', but the shift in vocabulary is obvious.

Notice though, the academic code of school isn't *just* about 'big words' (although longer words, with Latin and Greek roots, prefixes and suffixes are indeed more common in academic talk). It is much more about the complexity and density of meaning in those words used. Trying to simplify teacher talk to make it easily understood for our students is a fool's errand. Instead, we need to give them the keys to the academic code. We can practice academic talk daily in the classroom, and in writing, repeatedly until it becomes habitual.

Primarily, teacher talk needs to model, guide and instruct academic talk and vocabulary use. As Amy Benjamin, an American reading expert, sagely states:

As teachers, we should be using vocabulary we suspect (or know) that our students don't quite know yet, but we surround the unknown word with comprehensible input. If speaking this way becomes a habit, then our students are fortunate: they will be learning new words effortlessly.

*Infusing vocabulary into the reading-writing workshop,* by Amy Benjamin, p. 19

Benjamin goes on to recommend using examples, visuals and other strategies to hook in our student's background knowledge and existing word-hoard. The recommendation to "weave higher-level word choices" into our teacher talk is something that great teachers do intuitively, but given the primacy of vocabulary in determining the complexity of what children study and learn in school, it makes sense to plan to do this explicitly in our lesson planning, explanations and general classroom talk.

Rather than be directed by the volume of teacher talk, we should focus on the 'quality' of teacher talk. For example, we can weave higher-level word choices into our teacher talk with academic discourse markers to organise what we say: '*however* the audience could challenge the idea of Hamlet as a dramatic hero. *Alternatively,* the audience may perceive Hamlet as ...'. Simple word choices, such as using the more precise academic term 'perceive' instead of 'see', become absorbed into our children's word-hoards over time. We can respond to a student's answer with a clear enhancement of their initial word choices:

*Student:* They're guessing what will happen.
*Teacher:* OK, so the playwright uses foreshadowing to generate questions from the audience. What questions are the audience asking?

We can habitually model the shift from more restricted everyday talk to more sophisticated academic talk.

79

When children learn to automatically switch codes, moving from their everyday talk with friends and family, to using the academic code of school in more formal contexts, children possess one of the essential tools to flourish in their future lives. EAL students who are taught the academic code can become expert in code breaking and code switching, experienced as they are in negotiating different languages and switching between them. Children who had formally felt inadequate in the classroom, due to their limited vocabulary, develop the confidence to go on to succeed.

Ultimately, we can help bridge the vocabulary gap with rich, academic talk. Vocabulary here becomes a tool of power and privilege. Much debate has attended the 'restricted codes' of the academic world, our professions and our seats of power. Limited vocabulary can exclude us from that power structure. I am not saying our everyday language does not have power and great value, only that we should not be gated from the corridors of power because we cannot crack the entry code when we choose to do so.

As we know, how we say those words – our accent – as well as our gender, our class, nationality and race, can see us excluded from those symbolic corridors. By helping our children broaden their vocabulary, we do not end social inequality and the unfair exclusions that beset our class-ridden country, but we do make a start. We make a first step. It could prove a crucial first step in changing society for the better, breaking down barriers of communication that can separate us.

## The difference between the words we say and the words we read

Early language development and vocabulary growth for our children "floats on a sea of talk".[6] Remember the massive 30-million word gaps observed in homes before children even get to school? Still, it is crucial to recognise that academic talk alone will not close the vocabulary gap in our classrooms, particularly for older students.

No matter how well we model, scaffold and encourage academic talk in our classrooms, our talk simply won't prove as complex as the language of what our children read. Put simply, the older children become, the more how they talk becomes less like what they read.

The facts are stark: even children's books have 50% rarer words than the likes of the language of television, or even the conversation of graduates.[7] If reading a children's book is more complex than pretty much every type of adult talk, except the dialogue of the courtroom, this should give us the impetus to put an emphasis on improving academic reading in our schools.

Take this representative passage from a new GCSE Chemistry textbook:

Making polysaccharides from sugars

Monosaccharides can bond together to make larger molecules. For example, sucrose is made from a glucose and a fructose molecule bonded together (via a condensation reaction in which $H_2O$ is lost when making the link).

The monosaccharide sugars can also act as the monomers to make polymers, called polysaccharides. This can be made up of thousands of sugar monomers. Figure 4 shows simplified structures of starch and cellulose, both made up from glucose monomers joined in condensation polymerisation.

*Chemistry*, Third Edition, AQA (Oxford), p. 172

This is no elaborate trick to pick out a particularly tricky passage. **Remember the dead dodo passage in Chapter 1?** Try it yourself by opening a school textbook at random.

What you can see from the passage provided is that there is a highly technical style to a lot of academic language. The sophisticated nouns are clustered into expanded noun phrases, like "a glucose and a fructose molecule", "condensation reaction" and "monosaccharide sugars". Most of these noun phrases are an example of '**nominalisation**'. This is an integral grammatical feature of academic vocabulary and texts. Nominalisation is the process by which verbs or adjectives become nouns, usually by adding a suffix, for example, the verb 'condense' becomes the noun 'condensation'; the verb 'react' becomes the noun 'reaction'. The common use of nominalisation helps to create the passive and more abstract style of academic writing. So, for example, 'gas condenses into a liquid' becomes 'condensation'. Through this compression of meaning, an entire scientific process becomes clear.

The compression of language is useful to describe complex processes with clarity and precision, but it makes for tricky, abstract reading. Even describing these linguistic technicalities is hard work!

Now, it is true that in academic subjects like science, just because you know the name of the thing – the fancy noun phrase – it doesn't mean you deeply understand the 'thing'. Still, if you cannot even access the name of the 'thing', then you will have little hope of reaching towards understanding. Subject specific vocabulary here then provides both the first hurdle and the gateway to better understanding the science of making polysaccharides from sugars.

These elaborate names for scientific substances and processes are often unfamiliar to children, but they can prove relatively easy to learn because they typically have a singular meaning. In subjects like science, words are helpfully laden with common Latinate and Greek roots, prefixes and suffixes that reveal their meaning. Take "glucose" from the passage above. The word 'glucose' is one of those technical words that are used more broadly. Students may have seen it in the supermarket isle, with it repeated in science and the food technology classroom. From the Greek 'gleukos', meaning 'sweet wine', the 'cose' suffix is clearly common in the simple sugars in the passage: "glu<u>cose</u>", "fruct<u>ose</u>", "suc<u>rose</u>" and "cellul<u>ose</u>", another carbohydrate.

In recognising 'glucose', a word that is more likely part of the background knowledge of children in our classroom, we have a hook into classifying a whole family of words and related meanings. When we teach academic vocabulary then, we should seek out word families, as well as **synonyms** (words that have same meaning or very similar) and **antonyms** (words that have the opposite meaning). By doing so, we strengthen the connections that relate words, increasing the likelihood that they will be remembered. The human brain is a pattern-making machine, and this is true of how we remember words.

It is important to also recognise that informational texts – like the aforementioned chemistry textbook example – are very different to the fictional stories that most children have grown up reading. Academic vocabulary, as described, is full of nominalisations and polysyllabic words with Latinate and Greek prefixes and suffixes. There are also academic words like 'area', 'force' and 'moment', which have very specific meanings that require subject knowledge. By contrast, fictional stories have an emphasis on adjectives, adverbs and verbs to describe characters, settings and emotions.

Take these two famous opening lines:

It was a bright cold day in April, and the clocks were striking thirteen.

*1984*, by George Orwell[8]

As Gregor Samsa awoke one morning from uneasy dreams he found himself transformed in his bed into a monstrous vermin.

*Metamorphosis*, by Franz Kafka[9]

It is the adjectives "bright", "cold", "uneasy" and "monstrous" that carry much of the sinister meanings that are so important to convey the authors' meanings here. The nouns "thirteen" and "vermin" are not necessarily complex, but they have subtle layers of meaning that a reader considers. Children can rely on their long-standing knowledge of story genres, with their familiar beginning, middle and endings, to unpick such layers of meaning.

Similarly, a historical source can share the same active voice and familiar narrative elements of the fiction openings described. For example, a first-person account from the D-Day beach landing at Omaha beach can prove very familiar in style and relatively undemanding in terms of vocabulary:

Our assault boat hit a sandbar. I looked over the ramp and we were at least seventy-five yards from the shore, and we had hoped for a dry landing. I told the coxswain, "Try to get in further". He screamed he couldn't. That British seaman had all the guts in the world but couldn't get off the sandbar. I told him to drop the ramp or we were going to die right there.

This eyewitness account appears in: *June 6, 1944: The voices of D-Day*, by Gerald Astor, p. 4

Here, the word choices are not particularly academic, though "assault", "sandbar" and "coxswain" have specific meanings that may be outside of most students' background knowledge. The meaning of the passage – the dramatic action – is still not obscured. The metaphor "had all the guts in the world" brings a vivid and concrete description to add sense to this primary source. In history, for a text like this, the challenge is more related to corroborating the viewpoint in the text, sifting its meaning and comparing it with other accounts from the event. Children are able to build a 'story' for the event (remember those crucial *'mental models'*?).

Though promoting reading for pleasure is valuable and important for cracking the academic code, we should be aware that the vocabulary and style of fiction is typically very different to many of the non-fiction informational texts so commonly read in the school curriculum. Combining these different text types for a given topic is of course useful, thereby helping children recognise those important patterns and relationships between words and texts.

We know that well into the first years of secondary school, children's listening comprehension exceeds their ability to read complex words and texts. Knowing this, we should consider how we can read complex academic texts aloud wherever possible, probing the vocabulary knowledge and understanding of children in our classrooms. It is another example of the importance of 'word consciousness'. Here, the teacher needs to be acutely conscious of the degree of challenge of each and every text they use in their classroom.

Lots of people have attempted to define academic language in a way that is widely understood. William Nagy and Dianna Townsend have done a helpful job in describing *'words as tools'*, and have created a list of the six common features to describe typical academic language:[10]

1  A high proportion of Latin and Greek vocabulary.
2  A high proportion of complex words that have complex spellings.
3  A high proportion of nouns, adjectives and prepositions.
4  A high proportion of expanded noun phrases and nominalisation.

5  A high degree of informational density, i.e. few words that carry lots of meanings.
6  A high degree of abstraction, i.e. words that are removed from the concrete here and now.

Points 1 and 2 are of course related and need no more explanation. Point 3 shows how we use more nouns in academic talk, rather than relying on the here and now hints and nudges of everyday talk. This relates to point 4 and the use of expanded noun phrases, usually in the form of nominalisations. These nouns and expanded noun phrases are denser with information (point 5) and more abstract (point 6). These six common features describe how academic language is hard to understand and to learn.

Nagy and Townsend helpfully describe the abstract language used in academic talk or similar texts:

> A math text, for example, might contain abstract nouns such as length, width, circumference, addition, and subtraction. A biology text might contain abstract nouns for processes, such as respiration or mitosis.[11]
>
> *Words as tools: Learning academic vocabulary as language acquisition,* by William Nagy and Dianna Townsend, p. 94

Children can easily dismiss such 'fancy talk', but without the capacity to talk, read and write with an awareness of the qualities of academic language, even if some of it remains intuitive, their school success can be stunted. As the saying goes, language is power, with academic language proving the language of the powerful.

## What academic words should we choose to teach?

We know that different subject disciplines have different types of academic texts. We also know that there are different word families and words that are uniquely related to specific subjects. But what words should we devote the time to teach? Are some words more important to reading and the academic school curriculum than others?

Choosing what words we select to teach and those we choose to neglect is important for both curriculum design and lesson planning. Helpfully, linguistic experts have thought long and hard about how to best organise academic vocabulary, charting which words prove more important to reading and the academic code of school.

Isabel Beck and her colleagues, the authors of a seminal work on vocabulary, *Bringing words to life*, suggest a very helpful three-tier hierarchy for words we should teach in the classroom. Their three tiers of vocabulary are as follows (see Figure 4.1).

**Tier 1** words are the basic words of everyday talk – like 'people', 'good' or 'other' (see 'Appendix 3: The 100 most commonly used words in the English language'). These words are learned implicitly and do not require explicit teaching for most children. **Tier 2** words, by contrast, are valuable words that appear across the school curriculum, but they are not typically in everyday talk.

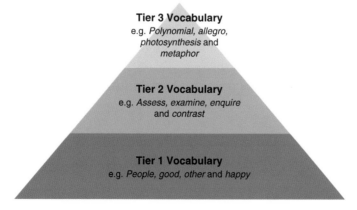

*Figure 4.1   Bringing words to life* – three tiers of vocabulary

Tier 2 vocabulary is essential to cracking the academic code. Beck and her colleagues strongly recommend the explicit teaching of *Tier 2* words. Take an important text from English history that many children will read at some stage of their education: 'The Magna Carta'. This short extract[12] from the famous charter is a warning to would-be criminals:

All evil customs relating to forests and warrens, foresters, warreners, sheriffs and their servants, or riverbanks and their wardens, are at once to be investigated in every county by twelve sworn knights of the county, and within forty days of their enquiry the evil customs are to be abolished completely and irrevocably. But we, or our chief justice if we are not in England, are first to be informed.

Magna Carta, 1215

We would be confident that children knew the meaning of "evil", though the emphasis on religion here may prove useful to a teacher. The *Tier 2* words here would likely prove to be "investigated", "enquiry", "abolished" and "irrevocably". As 'investigated' and 'enquiry' are interchangeable, we may clarify that they are understood, but it may be 'enquiry' that we explore in greater depth. We may make clear distinctions between 'enquiry' and 'inquiry', before giving a student-friendly definition and examples of the word in use. By pre-planning what words will need clarification, pre-teaching and highlighting as we read, we can help build up an assured hoard of *Tier 2* academic words.

The qualities of *Tier 2* words are not fixed or exact. Words like 'abolished' and 'irrevocably' do prove to be sophisticated alternatives to *Tier 1* words like 'end/stop' or 'final' and they typically have the prefixes and suffixes so commonly described in this book. We could no doubt help enrich children's academic talk and writing by focusing on using *Tier 2* vocabulary, such as using 'enquiry' in a literature essay (e.g. 'The audience is left to *enquire* about the intentions of the Inspector'). Indeed, in *An inspector calls*, a popular English Literature set text, the central character of the Inspector states: "One person and one line of *enquiry* at a time. Otherwise there's a muddle".[13]

*Tier 2* words frequently reappear in texts across the curriculum and they are very (or should I say *eminently?*) usable in children's own academic writing. For example, in history, slavery may have been '*abolished irrevocably* in the United States'; or in art, 'Art may have been *irrevocably changed* by Pablo Picasso in the twentieth century'; in geography, 'certain regions of the rainforest may be *irrevocably abolished* without significant government intervention'.

The final tier in Beck and colleagues' hierarchy are **Tier 3** words. These words are what we simply label subject specific vocabulary. This tier would include words like 'photosynthesis', 'polysaccharides' and 'nucleus' in science, or 'melody', 'tone' and 'allegro' in music. They are the words that teachers usually pay attention to in their day-to-day teaching, though perhaps without the 'word depth' described so far in this book. School textbook chapters can include numerous *Tier 3* words, helpfully highlighting them and organising them into a glossary.

Though teachers and textbooks typically foreground *Tier 3* vocabulary, it can be the *Tier 2* vocabulary that makes sense of the specialist *Tier 3* words. It is important then that if we are selecting texts of our own to use in the classroom that we pay careful attention to the *Tier 2* and *Tier 3* words that our students have to negotiate and understand to crack the academic code.

You may have noted that the categorisation of some of the *Tier 2* words above could provoke healthy debate. Though 'melody' and 'tone' have the subject specific qualities of *Tier 3* words in music, they are both words that I would use in the English literature classroom. Other common *Tier 3* academic words like 'area' (maths) and 'energy' (science) have more general *Tier 2*-like qualities. Of course, any such debate is entirely healthy and a great example of 'word consciousness'. If we plan our curricula and schemes of learning with this mode of thinking, good things would undoubtedly happen to the vocabulary development of our students.

Try it for yourself. Take a text you have used in the classroom this week, select an online article of note or even pluck a book from your bookshelf at random. Find a passage and begin allocating Beck's tiers to the vocabulary therein.

How many *Tier 2* words did you identify?

Did the number of *Tier 2* words correlate with the degree of reading difficulty of the text?

## Everyone loves a list

Another helpful selection of academic vocabulary has been selected for us. Avril Coxhead, in her 'Academic Word List' (AWL), has collated 570 word families (e.g. 'analysis' represents the wider family of 'analyse', 'analyses', 'analysed' and 'analyst') derived from over 3.5 million words from a range of university texts. Coxhead excludes the 2000 most common words in English and she includes only word families that appear at least 100 times.

The AWL is so useful because it effectively identifies some of the most essential *Tier 2* words for us. It has synthesised many of the academic words that appear in school textbooks, academic articles and more. Knowledge of the AWL is therefore a great aspirational target for children who aspire to academic success.

Let's look at the first 60 words from Coxhead's 'Academic Word List' in the following table:

| Analyse | Approach | Area | Assess | Assume | Authority |
|---|---|---|---|---|---|
| Available | Benefit | Concept | Consist | Constitute | Context |
| Contract | Create | Data | Define | Derive | Distribute |
| Economy | Environment | Establish | Estimate | Evident | Export |
| Factor | Finance | Formula | Function | Identify | Income |
| Indicate | Individual | Interpret | Involve | Issue | Labour |
| Legal | Legislate | Major | Method | Occur | Percent |
| Period | Policy | Principle | Proceed | Process | Require |
| Research | Respond | Role | Section | Sector | Significant |
| Similar | Source | Specific | Structure | Theory | Vary |

These words are of course familiar to us in schools. Many of these words are not just the most common academic words, but there are a fair few of the most common misspellings in there too!

See Appendix 4 Avril Coxhead's full 570-word 'Academic Word List' to survey the full list.

Coxhead's word list can be compared to the frequent exam command words now commonly shared by exam boards, with the obvious overlap between the two. We should be wary of merely wielding a word list stripped of their meaning in talk and reading, but if we begin by identifying the academic vocabulary of the school curriculum, we cannot help children begin to decipher and use those very words.

The AWL is the only useful word list we should consider. We can compose lists of common discourse markers that help organise academic writing too:

| Sequencing | Comparing | Contrasting | Qualifying |
|---|---|---|---|
| First (ly) | Similarly | Alternatively | However |
| Second (ly) | Likewise | Conversely | Although |
| Third (ly) | Like | On the other hand | But |
| Subsequently | In the same way | In contrast | Except |
| Finally | Equally | Instead | Notwithstanding |
| In conclusion | Akin to | Besides | Nonetheless |

### Wot d'ya mean by academic vocabulary?

| Supporting | Emphasising | Exemplification | Time |
|---|---|---|---|
| Moreover | Significantly | For example | Meanwhile |
| Furthermore | Indeed | Such as | Since |
| Also | Notably | Illustrated by | Before |
| Additionally | Significantly | For instance | After |

Discourse markers are the cohesive glue of academic talk, reading and writing. For our students to successfully decipher what they read, they need to automatically use and recognise these words. If we address them across our school, repeatedly, we offer our students the opportunity to consolidate their word-hoard.

As individual teachers, and as groups of teachers across our schools, we can use these academic word lists and helpful heuristics (a heuristic is a 'rule of thumb'), like Beck's three tier vocabulary model, as valuable planning tools. You could use the online 'Academic Word List Highlighter', from Nottingham University (see here: http://bit.ly/2v3yoyu) to get a sense of how common academic words from the list appear in school texts. By way of example, if you place the previous paragraph into the AWL Highlighter, you see 'individual', 'defining', 'benefits' and 'identify' emerge as words from Coxhead's useful list.

We should ask:

What are the essential *Tier 3* words for each topic?

Then, crucially, we have the following question:
How will we teach *Tier 2* and *Tier 3* words with the necessary 'word depth' so that every child in our school can crack the academic code?

Answering these questions gives us the strategy to begin to close the vocabulary gaps in our classroom.

## IN SHORT...

- The distinctive and important differences between 'everyday talk' and 'academic talk' too often remains implicit in school. We need to ensure that children understand these 'codes', code switching and code breaking when necessary.
- Academic language is typically characterised by complex and abstract words that are dense with information.
- Beck and colleagues offer a helpful shortcut to categorise academic vocabulary: *Tier 1* (everyday words); *Tier 2* (important academic words used frequently across the school curriculum); and *Tier 3* (subject specific vocabulary). We can use this to analyse texts in our school and select appropriate words to teach.
- Avril Coxhead's 'Academic Word List' offers a useful tool as it identifies the most common words in university texts that are also common in school texts and academic talk. Though not every child in our school will go to university, academic language characterises the voices of the powerful and that should be available to everyone.

## Notes

1   McKay, S. (26 August 2010). 'Telegraph crossword: Cracking hobby won the day – The boffins of Bletchley cut their teeth on the Telegraph crossword'. *The Telegraph.* Accessed online on 14 December 2017 at: www.telegraph.co.uk/lifestyle/well-being/7966268/Telegraph-crossword-Cracking-hobby-won-the-day.html.

2  Genesee, F., Lindholm-Leary, K., Saunders, W., & Christian, D. (2006). *Educating English language learners: A synthesis of research evidence.* Cambridge: Cambridge University Press.

3  Saunders, M., Goldenberg, C., & Marcelletti, D. (2013). 'English language development: Guidelines for instruction'. *American Educator*, Summer 2013.

4  Jackson, P. (30 March 2011). '100 words of English: How far can it get you?' BBC News website. Accessed online on 6 June 2016 at: www.bbc.co.uk/news/magazine-12894638.

5  This example was adapted from Hickey, P. J., & Lewis, T. (2015). 'To win the game, know the rules and legitimise the players: Disciplinary literacy and multilingual learners'. *The Language and Literacy Spectrum*, 25: 18–28.

6  Britton, J. (1970). *Language and learning.* Coral Gables, FL: University of Miami Press, p. 164.

7  Cunningham, A. E., & Stanovich, K. E. (1998). 'What reading does for the mind'. *American Educator*, 22 (1–2): 8–15.

8  Orwell, G. (1949). *1984.* London: Penguin Books.

9  Kafka, F. (Translation, 2007). *Metamorphosis and other stories.* London: Penguin Books.

10 Nagy, W., & Townsend, D. (2012). 'Words as tools: Learning academic vocabulary as language acquisition'. *Reading Research Quarterly*, 47 (1): 91–108. doi:10.1002/RRQ.011.

11 Ibid, p. 94.

12 This extract is taken from an English language translation of the Magna Carta from the British Library Website (published 28th July 2014). Accessed online on 9 August 2017 at: www.bl.uk/magna-carta/articles/magna-carta-english-translation.

13 Priestley, J. B. (Reprinted in 2000). *An inspector calls and other plays.* Penguin: London.

# 5 Developing vocabulary and 'disciplinary literacy'

What teacher could argue that language is not the tool of tools? What we call 'knowledge' is language, and this fact proves that to understand any subject, we need to first understand its language.

But it is a little more complicated than that. We know that the vocabulary of English is words, words, words, but then in science, geography and mathematics, you encounter a *'language'* that encompasses visual symbols, graphs, charts and diagrams. If we neglect these important differences in vocabulary and communication, then we threaten to alienate a large number of teachers who quickly deem teaching with vocabulary in mind as something for teachers in classrooms different to theirs.

Indeed, with curriculum time always proving to be at a premium in schools, with new qualifications and assessments proving ever-present at every phase of education, the notion of devoting time to vocabulary instruction appears to be impractical and foolhardy for too many teachers. Part of the problem with this focus on vocabulary and language is that it is lumped in with 'literacy across the curriculum'. Too often, in secondary schools in particular, the mention of 'literacy across the curriculum' is often accompanied by muffled groans. 'Why is this relevant to science, or music, or art or maths?' is the whisper. For a significant number of teachers, it is seen as a waste of their precious time.

The beleaguered literacy coordinator proves too commonly like a modern-day Sisyphus. They push the literacy boulder up the hill like an annual rite. They are kept busy by the demand for literacy targets and complex plans. They rattle out audits and stack up data in spreadsheets. The matter of 'literacy' really is a boulder of gargantuan proportions, beyond the will of any individual leader. There is a lack of teacher knowledge and confidence that is in part responsible for this state of affairs, but there are also beliefs evident from colleagues in the staffroom that 'literacy across the curriculum' is a little bit artificial and separate from how they should teach.

Geoff Barton, in his excellent book *Don't call it literacy!*, made an essential point about our attempts at enacting literacy across the curriculum. By labelling up the academic language of school and the means of communicating our curriculum as 'literacy', we wrongly offer it up as something extraneous, to be done in the corner of training days or to begrudgingly audit during the flagging final weeks of the summer.

What we then see is 'literacy' becoming compartmentalised into a narrow range of subject areas like English, history and modern foreign languages. The paradox here is that children are more likely to be exposed to new and unfamiliar vocabulary in science as much as they are in English literature. A comparison here from science is helpful:

> When someone does not understand one word or even a whole sentence in a page of a Harry Potter book, for example, it still makes sense and you can understand the story in the book. But when you do not understand a few words or even a single word on a page of chemistry

text, or in an examination question, it may not make sense and may lead to misunderstanding the concept.

*The role of language in the teaching and learning of chemistry*, by Peter Childs et al., p. 2[1]

When we begin to see each subject discipline as having their own language that children must learn, we begin to emphasise how important the academic code of school is to children. It offers teachers an approach to close the vocabulary gap for children with a restricted vocabulary (including EAL children), but every child benefits when we place such a focus on academic vocabulary and communication.

Put simply, the whole-school issue of literacy is too big and unwieldy, so we should instead shrink the problem down into something that teachers can manage and find meaningful. The answer: focus on vocabulary!

## What is disciplinary literacy and why is it important to every teacher?

There is a need to shift our thinking from seeing vocabulary, or indeed literacy more broadly, as a generic tool that we can apply in every classroom in the same way. The vocabulary of different subject areas has nuanced differences and how we think, speak, read and write as a historian, or a scientist or a mathematician, has some crucial differences that we must recognise. This perspective on literacy and vocabulary is best termed as '**disciplinary literacy**'.[2]

Our more conventional notion of literacy – we can call it '**content literacy**' – can indeed offer us lots of useful and useable strategies to help children better learn and understand how to best talk, read and write in school and beyond. I am not proposing we throw the metaphorical baby out with the bathwater. For example, we may choose to use reading strategies across different subject disciplines. **Reading comprehension strategies** are proven and offer us a framework for reading successfully. Such strategies include:

- **Prediction**: pupils predict what might happen as a text is read. This causes them to pay close attention to the text, which means they can closely monitor their own comprehension.
- **Questioning**: pupils generate their own questions about a text in order to check their comprehension.
- **Clarifying**: pupils identify areas of uncertainty, which may be individual words or phrases, and seek information to clarify meaning.
- **Summarising**: pupils describe succinctly the meaning of sections of the text. This causes pupils to focus on the key content, which in turn supports comprehension monitoring. This can be attempted using graphic organisers that illustrate concepts and the relationships between them using diagrams.
- **Inference**: pupils infer the meaning of sentences from their context and the meaning of words from spelling patterns.
- **Activating prior knowledge**: pupils think about what they already know about a topic, from reading or other experiences, and try to make links. This helps pupils to infer and elaborate, fill in missing or incomplete information and use existing mental structures to support recall.

## *Improving Literacy in Key Stage Two,* by the Education Endowment Foundation[3]

Such general approaches to tackling language from a traditional *'content literacy'* approach are based on good evidence, but they do need skilful application from teachers.

Children being able to develop their own reading strategies is helpful because they have to solve lots of different problems. They read in every subject. To exemplify, making predictions is a strategy a good reader would undertake when reading a novel, or a scientist when devising a hypothesis and a scientific test. Clearly, predictions in different disciplines have nuanced differences, but the shared language can be helpful to children who are developing their reading skills.

In history, a would-be-historian would ask **questions** about a text with a very specific purpose of evaluating whether the source is reliable, corroborating evidence and viewpoints across similar sources. Then they could **summarise** their reading of the different sources using a chronological perspective. What we begin to characterise here is *'reading like a historian'*.[4] This is the stuff of *'disciplinary literacy'* and it is a positive extension of a lot of good literacy practices undertaken in schools to date.

Approaches to developing vocabulary can be common across the curriculum too, with a focus on 'word consciousness' being adaptable and useful for every subject discipline. We know that words from the 'Academic Word List' can transcend subject boundaries, forming a more general 'academic code'.

When we begin to dig deeper into vocabulary learning, we see how subject disciplines emphasise different word groups for different purposes and this can prove crucial for successful learning.

We can devise a model for disciplinary literacy that we can apply to reading academic texts, as shown in Figure 5.1.

Subsequently, we can begin then to look at vocabulary from a more precise 'disciplinary literacy' perspective. Here is just a sample of insights as to how teaching vocabulary may differ to best support thinking, speaking, reading and writing in a range of subject disciplines in different ways.

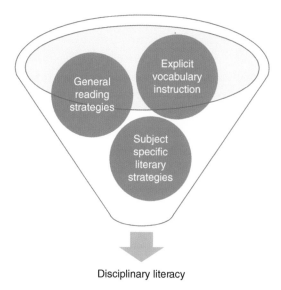

*Figure 5.1*   The disciplinary literacy model

## *Music*

In music, you have a breadth of Italianate words that dominate the discipline because of the origins of modern music. Therefore, you have words like 'aria', 'soprano', 'falsetto', 'tempo', 'allegro', 'crescendo', 'diminuendo', 'staccato', 'vibrato' and many more predominate. This family of Italian words offers meaningful opportunities for developing the relationships between the words, their roots and common word parts. Ultimately though, thinking like a musician is about quickly translating the specialist language into a soundscape. This swift interplay between language and its meaning in sound is unique to the discipline of music.

One music teacher colleague of mine, Tim Burnage, described a common opening to his lesson being '**Show me, show me**'. Children are given a musical term, before then having to enact the sound, offering memorable physical and oral cues to the meaning of the word.

**Acronyms**, a common vocabulary memorisation strategy, like *DR SMITH* (Dynamics, Rhythm, Structure, Melody, Instrumentation, Texture and Harmony), are widely used to categorise the many specialist words that describe the soundscape of music. Grouping and categorisation of vocabulary in music is such a common-sense approach given the vocabulary fits into such structures so logically. Take the 'D' of 'dynamics', where the disciplinary terms can be understood along a continuum:

- **Fortissimo**: very loud
- **Forte**: loud
- **Mezzo forte**: moderately loud
- **Mezzo piano**: moderately quiet
- **Piano**: quiet
- **Pianissimo**: very quiet

The words here can then be understood with something as simple as tapping upon the table, with the teacher verbally using statements to make clear the relationships between the words. When a child needs to describe unfamiliar music (a common GCSE assessment task), such musical terminology needs to be understood and used automatically, so that children can use it in their writing as they listen.

Of course, the notation of music is another related 'language' that children need to use and understand – making communication a little more complicated. Once more, we have the act of 'code switching' that proves to be essential for children to communicate in music and to navigate the academic world of school.

## *History*

In history, the important vocabulary children need to learn typically transcends national borders and easy categorisation. There are however categories that are more valuable than others in history. Given the concepts of time and change are so integral to understanding history, then related words are highly valuable and worth explicit teaching. Words like 'ancient', 'mediaeval', 'middle ages', 'modern', 'period', 'reign', 'Anno Domini', 'chronology', 'transitional', 'epoch', 'post-industrial' and 'calendar' are used repeatedly and so 'word depth' here is essential to thinking, speaking and writing like a historian.

A child reading a historical text may be looking to summarise a source, compare sources or seek out causes for historical events. This purpose requires 'reading like a historian', so it is important that vocabulary is seen through this lens. When a child writes like a historian, they are selecting from words that convey their interpretation of a primary or secondary source. From *Tier 2* words like 'suggests', 'implies' and 'infers', a child can navigate their way around the bloody tales and inherent biases of historical texts. Children can slip into dramatic storytelling when recounting and analysing historical texts, so understanding the academic code that sees nominalisation and the passive voice being commonly used is crucial.

Understanding history requires a vast array of background knowledge. The 'big picture' of historical periods is compressed into singular words like 'Renaissance' or 'mediaeval'. Knowing the name of the period does not mean that children know and understand a vast wealth of historical knowledge, but without first knowing the names of things we get nowhere. By giving explicit attention over to individual words we provide the 'mental Velcro' to learn and understand so much more. The value of unveiling the 1000-year history of a word of course is the stuff of the historian. Etymology needn't be a bolt on extra – it can be a potent tool for learning history.

## English literature

'Words, words, words'. It is the stuff of Hamlet and English literature. Curiously, we can teach a lot of English but not explicitly touch on words in great depth – their history, composite parts, groupings, idiosyncrasies and idioms.

From a technical perspective, in English literature, writers use such a broad sweep of words that any grouping or categorisation proves to be flawed. Still, we can recognise useful patterns. For example, in narratives, writers predominantly use adjectives to describe characters' actions and states of emotion. In their analytical essays, when a student in English literature selects from the words 'courageous', 'colossal' or 'audacious', they reveal different layers of understanding of a given character, action or theme. For this reason, *synonyms* are highly valued and they are the subject of a lot of teaching to enhance children's writing (in contrast to mathematics or science, where a precise and singular definition is all-important). Drawing upon a sophisticated range of words, especially adjectives, is then one of the chief factors that differentiate the best writers and the most sophisticated readers.

In analytical writing, students have to write in a sophisticated way about their reading. Students therefore also need to be comfortable using the sophisticated literary terms of literature and language study. This includes rhetorical devices, with Greek words like 'metaphor', 'asyndeton' and 'synecdoche'. These prove helpful in precisely defined literary language in use. We can go too far here with foregrounding such terminology. There is a tendency to fetishise the naming of things, with children labouring over learning long lists of fancy terms, but not really understanding the effects created by writers.

The vocabulary repertoire of children is integral to understanding great literature as well as informational non-fiction texts. At Key Stage Two, reading assessment focuses predominantly on **inference** – that is the exploring of layers of meaning within the writer's word choices – and this continues through to GCSE and beyond. 'Word depth' then proves the defining factor. In writing, vocabulary breadth and depth are equally decisive. Put simply, the best writers, typically drawing upon their vast store of 'mental models' of good generic writing, deploy an array of well-chosen words.

## Maths

The language of mathematics is wholly different to that of literary analysis or historical writing. The first, and most obvious, difference is that the special language of mathematics includes words, symbols, images and graphs.[5]

A typical maths teacher may rightly criticise spending a great deal of time on 'literacy across the curriculum' if it isn't made meaningful for their discipline. Now, every maths teacher knows that 'wordy' problems and clear logic both require students to grasp vocabulary and meaning with precision in maths. In their very own act of code switching, children are expected to translate problems with pizza slices into acute angles.[6] If we make the complex terminology understood automatically, children are free to then concentrate on their mathematical reasoning.

It is obviously valuable to have a deliberate plan for teaching Greek roots of numbers, like 'mono-', 'di-', 'tri-' and so on. It is also pretty much a necessity to pre-empt common misconceptions about mathematical vocabulary that has a broader use in general talk. And so, words like 'reflection', 'value' and 'absolute value' are defined and understood with their precise mathematical meaning. Children can quickly lose confidence in their mathematical skill and understanding when they face words that they thought they knew, given their everyday use – such as 'difference', 'prime' or 'product' – that now have an unfamiliar mathematical meaning.

The importance of *'speaking mathematically'* cannot be underestimated in supporting children's thinking and fending off misconceptions. The notion of mathematics as a "second language"[7] is therefore helpful in this regard. We should avoid the assumption that the language of mathematics is simply absorbed 'naturally' over time by children. It is this type of thinking that reinforces the notion that mathematics is not needed in daily life, or that algebra and maths theorems are meaningless. Instead, by making the 'second language' of mathematics more familiar and better understood by children, we can crack the tricky code of mathematics too.

## Science

Akin to mathematics, the origins of science are located in our classical Western academic tradition, so Greek and Latin root words are ever-present. Words, symbols, images and graphs all coalesce into a specialist code that can prove nearly inscrutable for too many children in our schools. Take communicating the concept of 'energy':

> On the one hand, it can be the symbol E, the unit of the joule, the energy levels in a graph or a mathematical equation to calculate the work done when a force moves through a distance; all of these are simply different representations of the same concept ... Given such complexity, is it any surprise that the act of explaining science is so problematical?
>
> 'Effective strategies for teaching science vocabulary', by Sarah J. Carrier[8]

Alongside this *Tier 3* vocabulary, we have evidence that the main problem in science is how *Tier 2* vocabulary is used in different ways in science.[9] Words like 'account', 'achieve', 'characteristic', 'component', 'conserve', 'denote', 'derive', exert', 'interpret', 'random', 'relative' 'release', 'uniform' and 'variation'[10] all prove to be common barriers for understanding science. And yet, despite the obvious challenges for children trying to access important scientific language, vocabulary is seldom explicitly taught in the science classroom.[11]

In science teaching and learning, we see categories of vocabulary across the different disciplines of physics, chemistry and biology. Within and across those disciplines, we have categories of *Tier 3* and *Tier 2* vocabulary overlapping with graphs, symbols, diagrams and mathematical equations. Given this complexity, the importance of 'word depth' and a strong focus on 'word consciousness' is nowhere more important than the science classroom. Everyday talk is always transformed in science into the academic code of school: 'bacteria splitting in two' becomes 'binary fission'. The language of science requires constant mediation and translation if we are to help close the vocabulary gap in our science classrooms.

The Education Endowment Foundation and Oxford University have drawn together a wealth of research[12] that shows that children from disadvantaged backgrounds don't continue with science after the age of 16 (when it is no longer compulsory). Of course, this has lots of complex causes, but the link between the reading comprehension of such students and their success in science is inextricable. Reading, knowing and understanding the complex vocabulary of science may well translate to helping to bridge the gap for many children into a career in science.

## MFL

Vocabulary knowledge is most obviously paramount in the learning of a modern foreign language. The act of translation is not implicit-like in the science classroom – it is explicit and dominant. Most people have had the frustrating experience of trying to communicate in a foreign country, but the essential word just won't appear on the tip of your tongue. You can struggle to communicate without knowledge of French or German grammar, but you cannot communicate at all without a wealth of words.

There has been a great deal of debate in the English education system of the value of learning new languages. The teaching of languages is described as being in a "fragile state", with fewer than half of children in England taking a GCSE in a language.[13] My book is explicit in promoting language, broadening and deepening our children's knowledge of English, and there is little doubt that one of the keys to unlock learning for children taking on an additional language is an assured and deep knowledge of one's home language. Closing the vocabulary gap then could do a great deal to support and bolster the 'fragile state' of languages in our school system.

Now, my emphasis on vocabulary and learning is proverbial egg sucking for teachers of languages. It is their daily business. They know well that there are disciplinary differences that relate to different languages, as the likes of Spanish has a 'shallow orthography' – where the letters (graphemes) and sounds (phonemes) match consistently – and it also has a more straightforward grammatical system compared to the likes of French. Given such language differences, exploring differences in 'disciplinary literacy' is again valuable.

The learning of all additional languages is best rooted in a broad and deep English vocabulary. One reason why good English vocabulary breadth and depth matters so much is the many **cognates** that help children recognise unfamiliar foreign words. Cognates are words that are obviously related across languages, like 'gratitude' in English being a cognate with 'gratitudo' in Spanish. MFL teachers are acutely aware that there are 'false cognates' that confuse children, but that generally recognising cognates across languages is highly beneficial for learning an additional language. For example, 'ancient' in English is commonly used to denote something or someone being very old, whereas 'ancien' in French commonly denotes former, such as 'l'ancien joueur' – 'the former player'. These 'false friends' need addressing and is a recognised part of MFL 'disciplinary literacy'.

Teaching vocabulary by topic or in lists is common, given taking on a vast number of words and their meaning in a short space of time is imperative to success for children learning a new language. Knowing an array of nouns however has obvious limitations and some topics, say sports, offer up specialist words that can prove a little too niche and are unlikely to be repeated. A topic glossary, or word list, can lack the required grammar knowledge, such as different verb forms, or the nuanced multiple meanings of words. When we deal in MFL word lists to practice, we miss subtleties of pronunciation, like stress, rhythm and intonation, which are essential to speaking in an additional language. Communicating with words takes repeated exposures to talk, listening, reading and writing in the target language to bring word lists to life.

It is estimated that a child can read most school-based French or Spanish reading materials with a second language word-hoard between 8000 and 9000 words, with fluent speech requiring up to 7000 words.[14] A crucial aspect of learning an additional language is developing 'word depth'. A narrower focus on vocabulary is viable and pragmatic if we select the most apt words. Then being exposed, repeatedly, to rich talk and challenging reading adds 'word depth', seeing children develop a more nuanced understanding of those words.

There is so much more to say about developing vocabulary through subject disciplines, but they are beyond the bounds of this short book and the parameters of my narrow subject knowledge. Expert teachers, knee-deep in communicating their subject on a daily basis, need to talk about vocabulary and how to teach it better in their own disciplinary terms. Vocabulary development does not exist in a vacuum: it is a means to better communicate as a geographer, a linguist or as a writer. For teachers of all phases, we are left with important and useful questions to drive our understanding of 'disciplinary literacy' and vocabulary development forward:

- What is the essential vocabulary of **X** subject discipline?
- What are the similarities and differences between communicating in subject discipline **X** compared to other subject disciplines?
- Are there any common misconceptions and confusion between words in discipline **X** compared to other subjects, or with words in more general use (words like 'energy' in science)?
- What does a child need to **know**, **do** and **understand** to **talk**, **read** and **write** like [insert subject discipline requiring this knowledge, e.g. historian, computer scientist or mathematician]?

Seeing vocabulary development through a lens of disciplinary knowledge and understanding is essential for teachers of older children at secondary school in particular, as the academic language of this phase changes so substantially from children's everyday talk, becoming so much more specialist and complex. And yet, at every phase, it is a useful activity to better promote vocabulary development.

We must recognise that primary schools are not necessarily organised into subject disciplines, and although most secondary schools are organised in this way, a great deal of training for teachers is still conducted centrally so that generic approaches to literacy and vocabulary dominate. Of course, beginning with what we know more generally about vocabulary development is both important and practical, but we should then consider how we can go on to adapt our focus more specifically in subject areas and for different phases in school. In primary schools and secondary schools, we can balance general approaches to vocabulary learning, before channelling our approaches to more specialist disciplinary strategies as children progress through school.

## IN SHORT...

- Our traditional approach to literacy – we can label it *'content literacy'* – needs to be understood in relation to the more specific focus on subject-specific communication inherent in 'disciplinary literacy'. Generic approaches to vocabulary learning can, and should, complement 'disciplinary literacy'.
- General approaches to literacy, like reading comprehension strategies, can give us a shared language for learning, but they should still be combined with a nuanced application within specific subject disciplines.
- Different subject disciplines draw upon varied academic codes, with subjects like science and maths encompassing words, symbols, graphs and diagrams, whereas subjects like history, English and

MFL share a more 'traditional' diet of academic vocabulary.

- Some strategies for vocabulary development, like the study of morphology to better understand words and concepts, may prove more successful in subjects with a very high percentage of Greek and Latin root words, like science, compared to developing vocabulary in a subject like English literature, which may benefit more from an explicit focus on synonyms and antonyms.

- Every subject has its own 'language' and this code needs to be communicated to our novice students if they are going to flourish academically.

## Notes

1 Childs, P. E., Markic, S., & Ryan, M. C. (2015). 'The role of language in the teaching and learning of chemistry'. In J. García-Martínez & E. Serrano-Torregrosa (eds.), *Chemistry education: Best practices, opportunities and trends* (pp. 421–446). Weinheim: Wiley-VCH Verlag GmbH & Co. KGaA.

2 Shanahan, T., & Shanahan, C. (2008). 'Teaching disciplinary literacy to adolescents: Rethinking content-area literacy'. *Harvard Educational Review*, 78 (1): 40–59.

3 Education Endowment Foundation (2017). *Improving literacy in key stage two: Guidance report*. London: Education Endowment Foundation.

4 Reisman, A. (2012). 'Reading like a historian: A document-based history curriculum intervention in urban high schools'. *Cognition and Instruction*, 30 (1): 86–112.

5 O'Halloran, K. L. (2005) (Reprinted 2008). *Mathematical discourse: Language, symbolism and visual images*. New York, NY: Continuum.

6 Dunston, P. J., & Tyminski, A. M. (2013). 'What's the big deal about vocabulary?' *NCTM, Mathematics Teaching in the Middle School*, 19 (1) August.

7  Jones, B. R., Hopper, P. F., & Franz, D. P. (2008). 'Mathematics: A second language'. *Mathematics Teacher*, 102 (4): 307–312.
8  Carrier, S. J. (2011). 'Effective strategies for teaching science vocabulary'. Learn NC. Accessed online on 10 September 2016 at: www.learnnc.org/lp/pages/7079?ref=searchwww.learnnc.org/lp/pages/7079?ref=search.
9  Osborne, J., & Dillon, J. (2010). *Good practice in science teaching: What research has to say*. New York, NY: Open University Press, p. 141.
10  Tao, P. K. (1994). 'Words that matter in science: A study of Hong Kong students' comprehension of non-technical words in science'. *Educational Research Journal*, 9 (1): 15–23.
11  Wexler, J., Mitchell, M. A., Clancy, E. E., & Silverman, R. D. (2016). 'An investigation of literacy practices in high school science classrooms'. *Reading and Writing Quarterly*, 33 (3): 258–277.
12  Education Endowment Foundation and the University of Oxford (2017). 'Review of SES and science learning in formal educational settings: A report prepared for the EEF and the Royal Society'. London: Education Endowment Foundation. Accessed online on 27 September 2017 at: https://educationendowmentfoundation.org.uk/public/files/Review_of_SES_and_Science_Learning_in_Formal_Educational_Settings.pdf.
13  Teaching School Council (2017). 'Modern foreign languages pedagogy review: A review of modern foreign languages teaching practice in key stage two and key stage three'. Accessed online on 10 August 2017 at: www.tscouncil.org.uk/wp-content/uploads/2016/12/MFL-Pedagogy-Review-Report-2.pdf.
14  Schmitt, N., & Pellicer-Sánchez, A. (2010). 'Incidental vocabulary acquisition from an authentic novel: *Do things fall apart?*' *Reading in a Foreign Language*, 22 (1): 31–55.

# 6 We need to talk about spelling

Take care that you never spell a word wrong. Always before you write a word, consider how it is spelled, and, if you do not remember, turn to a dictionary. It produces great praise to a lady to spell well.

> Thomas Jefferson, American president:
> 1801 to 1809, to his daughter

It is a damn poor mind that can think of only one way to spell a word.

> Andrew Jackson, American president: 1829 to 1837

The breadth and depth of our vocabulary is always on display in our daily talk, from light conversation to professional presentations. Our word-hoard is also exhibited in our writing too, from off-hand text messages, to work emails or extended essays. Debates about the importance and value of spelling have raged for centuries and our capacity to spell accurately whenever we write matters as much as ever.

The social judgments that attend spelling are centuries old. You can see it on view at the beginning of the nineteenth century, with famed founding father and former American president Thomas Jefferson, guiding his daughter with genteel advice on the lady-like fashion of spelling words with accuracy. The implication: a lady and a gentleman convey something of their intelligence in their spelling ability and that such knowledge is praiseworthy. Andrew Jackson, another former president, only a few years later – well, he plays fast and loose with the rules – gentility be damned.

These polarised attitudes towards spelling have spanned the chequered history of our language, with as many happy rule breakers as conscientious rule makers. The debate about spelling rolls on, but regardless of our personal stance, there is still an important judgment made about the credibility of our words when we write them with accuracy or in error. Many students know this implicitly, often selecting words in our writing that we can spell with accuracy over a sophisticated word choice with a tricky spelling.

Can spelling then hamper our communication *and* our credibility?

Take the credibility of the present day American president, Donald Trump. He recently claimed to have "the best words", but his credibility is in question given his erratic spelling attempts on social media (and a lot more besides, to be fair): from "councel" instead of 'counsel'; "tapp" instead of 'tap'; "to" instead of 'too'; "attaker" and not 'attacker'; and even "educatuon" instead of 'education'. Of course, there is the enigmatic gem, "covfefe", baffling us all. Unless it is a clever ruse to exhibit the common mistakes that beset children in our schools – 'the best ruse' – then what Trump reveals is a shaky spelling knowledge and a limited grasp of the English language.

It is not uncommon for powerful people to lack spelling skill, but it is unsettling for most of us because, like Jefferson claimed of his contemporaries, we easily conflate intelligence with spelling ability. We confer credibility on those with a broad vocabulary that is communicated *accurately.* The story then of orthography – our conventional spelling system – is a very valuable one in all sorts of ways.

Heralded English wordsmiths like Jane Austen or Winston Churchill have famously struggled with their spelling. Being a great speaker or writer does not always align with being a successful spell checker. Unsurprisingly, if we are in possession of a broad and deep knowledge of vocabulary, we can be more confident in our spelling accuracy. With a deeper understanding of the vagaries of our English language spelling system, which sits alongside our developing knowledge of words, we offer a vital tool for children to develop into accurate and confident spellers.

With over 1 million words and some 1300 years of history of countless spelling shifts, it is rather predictable that spelling proves a complex challenge for children in our schools. Crucially, however, with better knowledge of vocabulary – 'word depth' – we offer spelling strategies that are robust and reliable. As Dr Louisa Moats, Vice President of the International Dyslexia Association, states:

> Virtually every word's spelling can be explained by its language of origin, meaning, and/or sound structure. Odd and truly unpredictable spellings, such as 'of', 'aunt' and 'does' are only a small percentage of words in English.
>
> 'How spelling supports reading',
> by Louisa Moats, p. 21[1]

We need to better support teachers and children to know more about the limitations of spelling rules and why recognising historical '*spelling patterns*' instead is an important distinction. We need to guide teachers to enact better spelling instruction. The reliance on spelling lists, 'look-cover-write-check' and the limited, and even potentially damaging, 'Friday spelling test',[2] are commonplace because teachers are seldom supported with training on how to teach such a specialist aspect of our language.

Spelling is always subject to change and debate. This chapter so far has cited Americans, which helps to highlight some common drivers of language change. We can see the global battle between English and American spellings over common words, such as 'manoeuvre' – or is it 'maneuver'? The American omission of the 'o' is a common simplification of the spelling and it is on the increase (the 'o' is a Latin influence, from 'operari', meaning 'to work'). Given the mouthful of vowels already present in a word so obviously tricky to spell, the small shift is obvious, but who enshrines this change? Who mandates the 'correct' spelling?

Debates over Americanisms and other linguistic tweaks are nothing new to the English language. Up until the sixteenth century, words like 'razor' were commonly spelled with an 's', until the 'z' eventually became commonplace. We are in the midst of unique spelling changes right now, like the common omission of 'h' in 'rhubarb' (unsurprisingly, another Latin legacy). If offers us an example of how our globalised technology is shifting our spelling patterns, changing and typically simplifying spellings.

Despite these shifts drawing our attention, they are in fact few and far between. We can design reliable, cumulative spelling programmes that offer every child the opportunity to exhibit skill in spelling with a good deal of confidence. We do need to support our children to have a better array of spelling strategies: from a deep knowledge of our linguistic history, a sound knowledge of the alphabetic code, an awareness of morphology and common spelling patterns and singular oddities to remember.

Putting all this simply, the more words you know, and the more you know about words, the better you become at spelling.

## Beyond 'spelling by rote' and towards 'spelling by reason'

The ubiquitous 'Friday spelling test' does have some place in our spelling instruction. The **'testing effect'** does help us to remember *some* important spellings, but if children do not understand *why* some spelling are as they are, recognising common and uncommon patterns, then they will never be fully equipped to write and spell effectively. Remembering so many words by sight, which is what most spelling tests encourage, is therefore an ineffective strategy.

Many teachers, like myself, have used spelling tests, but have bemoaned how those tested spellings were quickly forgotten. The weak effects of these 'test and learn' methods that are patently lacking meaningful knowledge are dispiriting for many teachers. I am optimistic that there is a better way.

Even good spellers benefit from sustained, explicit spelling instruction, such as focusing on morphology and etymology, to understand the reasoning behind many of our spelling patterns. As we know already, Latin has made an indelible impression on the English language and was favoured for much of the academic vocabulary we use today. Some spellings have simply preserved their Latin look in words, like 'torrid' and 'pallid'. With a little digging, you can observe distinct etymological histories that are bound to our common spelling patterns. Old Norse and Dutch spellings can be seen in 'skin' and 'skip', whereas Latin etymology affects comparable sounding words with a 'c', such as 'sceptic' and 'scornful'.

What is clear is that meaning, and the etymology of a word, can take precedence over the sounds. Therefore, it is tricky for children who try to relate the letter to sound correspondences that helped them *'learn to read'* (remember the phonics method in Chapter 2) for many of the academic words that they '*read to learn*' later on in school.

In words like 'subtle' and 'debt', there is the seemingly odd 'b' that has no place in the sounding out of the word. Both have derived the 'b' from the Latin origins of 'debitum' and 'subtilis'. Latin influences are also seen in words using the 'cede' suffix, from the Latin 'cedere', meaning 'to yield, give place; to give up some right or property'. We are left with confusing patterns, like 'succeed' and 'proceed', coexisting alongside 'recede' and 'procede'. The sound and letter correspondences in English – remember our 'deep orthography' – are what make learning English spelling much harder than many other languages.

Some of the reasons for spelling shifts in our linguistic history are specific and some downright annoying. Before agreed spellings were enshrined in dictionaries, scribes from the Middle Ages would commonly add letters into words just to ensure that the length of the lines on their beautiful decorated scripts were even. Adding an 'e' to words like 'have', 'give', 'live', 'groove', 'sneeze', 'gone' and 'done' was therefore a common solution. Spelling mistakes like 'hav' and 'gon' make perfect sense to a child at the '**phonetic stage**'[3] of spelling development. Of course, though important, sounding out words only gets you so far with our English orthography.

The rogue scribes didn't stop there in influencing our spelling system. They wrote in gorgeous handwriting, but this had a significant influence on modern spelling that still bedevil children, and adults, today. Take the spelling of the word 'love'. Why isn't it the phonetic form 'luv' like a million private phone messages? The answer, again, is buried in history. The scribes wrote using 'minims' – a simple downward stroke of a pen – I – for the letters 'i', 'j', 'n', 'u', 'v', 'm' and 'w'. With the spelling 'luv' you get a confusing jumble of minims – IIIII –, whereas with an 'o' you get greater visual clarity: IoIIe. With a bit of linguistic searching, you can see how variations like 'carry' have the plural form 'carries/carried', revealing the hidden past of carrie/carry spelling variations. Other patterns emerge, such as how words end in an 'i', for similar reasons, with 'y' becoming dominant.

When children write 'dying your hair' in error, or 'dieing' of embarrassment, they aren't going far wrong. In tripping over long-standing spelling patterns by mistake, they can unwittingly stumble into a linguistic history lesson, such as the general avoidance of using three consecutive vowels in words, for example, 'iei'. With some support and structured teaching of the historical reasoning for spelling, children further develop their 'word depth' and broaden their cultural knowledge too.

Spelling has been described as developing in stages,[4] with the 'phonetic stage' obviously matching their early reading instruction. Children then move on to an aptly titled **'transition stage'**, where they recognise word parts, visual patterns, etymological roots and more. When they begin to combine all of these strategies they progress to the final **'correct spelling stage'**, which describes exactly what it says on the tin.

The linguistics legend David Crystal, whose shared wisdom informs so much of this chapter and book, sagely stated:

> I find it hard to resist the conclusion that, if children were introduced to some basic etymology, many of the 'famous' spelling errors would be avoided.
> *Spell it out: The singular story of English spelling,*
> by David Crystal, pp. 266–267

Crystal recommends foregrounding the explicit teaching of etymology and morphology. He relates how common roots, like 'auto' (meaning 'self'), can quickly be understood through modelling sentences such as, 'The **au**thor signed his **auto**biography with a fancy **auto**graph'. He also explains compelling narratives around individual words that prove interesting and instructive, exciting a curiosity for vocabulary, spelling and grammar that is deeply memorable. Clearly, the Latin and Greek word roots, prefixes and suffixes in the previous chapter are not just tools to grow word knowledge and vocabulary, but also a method to develop spelling knowledge and accuracy.

My favourite example of a Crystal etymological tale is that of Wynkyn de Worde and the spelling of 'ghost'. Wynkyn was one of William Caxton's assistants – Caxton is most celebrated for bringing the printing presses to England and revolutionising reading – brought over to England from Holland as too few English people were up to the job of typesetting the new books. In the fifteenth century, with looser attitudes towards spelling, Wynkyn's Flemish heritage infiltrated the English language. The word 'ghost', then commonly spelled phonetically as 'gost', gained a 'silent h' from the Flemish spelling for ghost – 'gheest'. This 500-year-old error is now a mainstay in our lexicon, with ghastly consequences for some children's spelling!

Of course, we do not have the time, or necessarily the knowledge, to explore the spelling history of *every* word a child may encounter, but an explicit focus on etymological roots and word parts can change how a child thinks as they write and spell. It is powerful knowledge that makes the seeming oddities of the English language less daunting and it can see spelling infused with memorable meaning.

We should ask: what common spelling errors would be helped by a memorable exploration of where the word has come from?

For me, I would unpick 'metaphor' for my English teaching. It is a core concept in any study of literature and it is a word that is spelled badly by countless students I have taught. The etymology and word parts are straight forward: the Latin prefix 'meta', meaning 'over, across', and the Latin 'pherein', meaning 'carry, bear', are combined. To 'carry over' is then the meaning of the word. So the word 'metaphor' is itself metaphorical! Following this word story, getting children to generate as many words as they can with the 'meta' prefix is a handy start, even coining their own words. This could be followed by foregrounding words that have the 'ph' pairing to represent the 'f' sound (look out for more on these letter and sound correspondences later in the chapter).

Paying deliberate attention to the roots, history, words parts and correct spelling of individual words could potentially prove time-consuming, so selecting words judiciously for their high value, words that you want children to remember, is of course important. We should not ignore the reality that unpicking words can also be a very quick, seamless part of our everyday explanations. By foregrounding language daily in this way, we make 'word consciousness' a typical and habitual part of learning.

Spelling isn't incidental, it is deeply meaningful and offers children powerful knowledge. Clearly then, one worthwhile strategy that eases our reliance on the 'Friday spelling test' is exploring spellings with common word roots – like 'cred'. We just need to remember Donald Trump's questionable **cred**ibility that has left many people in**cred**ulous!.

Look again at the word roots and popular prefixes like those shared in Chapter 3 as a tool for teaching spelling.

## The problem with spelling rules

Why can't we just issue some cast-iron spelling rules and be done with it? Well, as you know, the English language, like those pesky scribes from the Middle Ages, has a history of rule-breaking that means we are better off seeking out patterns than trying to apply fixed rules.

Indeed, the most famous 'spelling rule' of them all – **'i' before 'e', except after 'c'** – is notoriously unreliable. There is some validity in the 'rule'. 'Believe' compared to 'deceive' is perhaps a helpful comparison that proves the 'rule'. And yet, the exceptions are legion and this can prove disheartening for children. It would certainly not be effective if you were looking to 'study the science of the species sufficiently'.

Now, if we take such common patterns and wed them to an awareness of etymology and morphology, then you can have a deeper grasp of such spelling patterns. We can delve into related patterns, like how most 'ei' spellings appear when an 'e' precedes a suffix beginning with 'i', such as 'atheism' or 'deity'. Spelling rules cannot be slavishly adhered to with much success. For many expert linguists, they are merely the remnants of a pedantic eighteenth-century class of commentators.

Children and teachers being in possession of spelling lists can often lead to superficial teaching and learning, where important patterns are not internalised, due to a shallow degree of knowledge about **why** spelling patterns occur, their variations and quirks.

Knowledge of grammar is certainly helpful for children looking to recognise consistent patterns for spelling academic words. *Inflections* – the change in the grammatical function of a word, for example, shifting the present tense 'walk' to the past tense 'walked' – offer us some useful guideposts for the ending of words, along with their variant spellings.

The following table shows some common inflection patterns that we can use to support children's spelling.

| Word type | Spelling pattern | Example |
|---|---|---|
| Verbs that end 'consonant – e' | Omit 'e' before adding 'ing' | Love – loving |
| Words ending with 'ie' | Change 'ie' to 'y', then add 'ing' | Die – dying |
| Words ending with 'o' | Add 'es' to the plural form | Volcano – volcanoes |
| Words ending 's', 'sh', 'ss', 'ch' | Add 'es' to the plural form | Push – pushes |
| Words ending 'ch' | Add 'es' to the plural form | Catch – catches |
| Words ending 'consonant – y' | Change 'y' to 'ie' before 's' ending | Try – tries |
| Words ending 'consonant – y' | Change 'y' to 'i' before 'est', 'ed', 'er' and 'ly endings | Try – tried Easy – easiest |
| Words ending 'consonant – y' | Don't change the 'y' before 'ing' ending | Try – trying |
| Words ending 'vowel – y' | Don't change the 'y' | Toy – toys |
| Single syllable words: 'consonant – vowel – consonant' | Double the final consonant before 'ed', 'est', 'er' and 'ing' endings | Shop – shopping Fat – fatter |
| Double syllable or more words: 'consonant – vowel – consonant' with stressed final syllable | Double the final consonant before 'ed', 'est', 'er' and 'ing' endings | Begin – beginning |
| Double syllable or more words: 'consonant – vowel – consonant' with stressed opening syllable | Don't double the final consonant before 'ed', 'est', 'er' and 'ing' endings | Follow – following |

Other patterns and non-patterns in the language emerge. By way of an example, you could give your students the near-Sisyphean task of finding words in English that end with the following letter: 'i', 'j', 'q', 'u' and 'v'. As ever, there are exceptions like 'chilli', 'Iraq', 'bureau' or 'you', of course, but the majority are infrequent loan words. Patterns of word endings, or non-patterns, are quite consistent and therefore prove useful word and spelling knowledge. You could go onto ask students to work out alternative endings to a sound like 'j', so that students can work out common alternatives like 'ju**dge**' or 'knowle**dge**'. Or they could pursue alternative endings for 'u', commonly observed in words like 'bl**ue**' and 'tr**ue**'. Children quickly develop an 'ear' for language and a visible memory for such spelling patterns.

Now, primary school teachers and children will be aware that working knowledge of the phonetic alphabet and phonics is vitally important here. For teachers of older children, phonics knowledge is often scant or non-existent.

As explained in Chapter 2, English has what is known as a 'deep orthography', meaning that individual sounds can be spelled in a variety of ways. For example, the consonant 'c' has the widest range of sounds of all the English consonants: 'k' – '<u>c</u>at'; 'q' – <u>c</u>ue; 's' – 'sin<u>c</u>e'; 'sh' – spe<u>c</u>ial; 'x' – a<u>cc</u>ess. The British Council phonemic chart[5] (using the International Phonetic Alphabet – IPA) is therefore a very handy resource for children of all ages, as it defines how different letters, and their spelling patterns, correspond to the sounds in the English language, as shown in the following table.

| Vowels | | Consonant | |
|---|---|---|---|
| IPA/sound | Examples | IPA/sound | Examples |
| /iː/ (ee) | Seat, green, tree, relief | /p/ (p) | Pull, stop, apple |
| /i/ (i) | Sit, grin, fish | /b/ (b) | Bet, about, beer |
| /ʊ/ (short oo) | Good, foot, pull | /h/ (h) | Hot, head, heart |
| /uː/ (long oo) | Food, rule, shoe | /f/ (f) | Four, food, fish |
| /e/ (e) | Head, bet, said | /v/ (v) | Observer, vow, vote |
| /ə/ (uh) | Teacher, observer, about | /m/ (m) | Money, lamb, my |
| /ɜː/ (er) | Girl, nurse, earth | /t/ (t) | Tree, stop, want |
| /ɔː/ (or) | Walk, door, four | /d/ (d) | Door, food, huddle |
| /æ/ (a) | Had, lamb, apple | /n/ (n) | Grin, green, nurse |
| /ʌ/ (u) | Cup, love, money | /θ/ (th) | Earth, thigh, throw (unvoiced) |
| /aː/ (ar/ah) | Heart, dark, fast | /ð/ (th) | They, there, bathe (voiced) |
| /ɒ/ (o) | Hot, stop, want | /ŋ/ (ng) | Sing, English, drank |
| **Diphthongs** | | /tʃ/ (ch) | Teacher, chair, choice |
| /ɪə/ (eer) | Year, beer, ear | /dʒ/ (j) | Joke, joy, lounge, ridge |
| /eə/ (air) | Chair, where, there | /r/ (r) | Rule, grin, tree |
| /əʊ/ (oh) | Joke, vote, throw | /s/ (s) | Stop, since, city, pseudonym |
| /aʊ/ (ow) | Vow, lounge, out | /z/ (z) | Observe, noise, president |
| /eɪ/ (ay) | They, bathe, way | /l/ (l) | Pull, love, rule |
| /aɪ/ (igh) | Thigh, dice, my | /ʃ/ (sh) | Shoe, fish, sure, pollution |
| /ɔɪ/ (oi) | Joy, noise, choice | /ʒ/ (zh) | Casual, measure, pleasure |
| | | /w/ (w) | Want, way, where |
| | | /k/ (k) | Walk, dark, cup, plaque |
| | | /g/ (g) | Green, grin, girl |
| | | /j/ (y) | Year, yes, yellow |

Making these sound–letter correspondences visible in every classroom can help children do a better job of dictionary searches for spellings. Such tools prompt not just 'word consciousness' in our students, but they can also inspire a unique sense of *'spelling consciousness'* too. 'Chunking' down words to their component parts is a common spelling strategy and one that is particularly useful when a child is faced with tricky, uncommon letter to sound correspondences, like the 'que' in 'plaque' or 'queue' (it helpfully foregrounds morphological analysis too). Such strategies, when taught habitually and consistently, can become automatic for our students.

So spelling rules often prove unreliable, but there are many strategies relating to the etymology of words, word parts, as well as the crucial letter–sound (grapheme–phoneme) relationship, that we can draw upon to support children's spelling. Still, however, the English language poses issues that render those strategies largely redundant! We come to the curious case of homophones and homographs:

- **Homophones**: a type of homonym that also sound alike and have different meanings, but also different spellings, for example, there/their/they're; pear/pair.
- **Homographs**: words that are spelled the same but have different meanings, for example, desert (a hot, arid region)/desert (to leave); evening (late afternoon)/evening (making things more even).

There are around 500 homophones in the English language, but given many are so commonly used, they appear more common than they actually prove to be. Given many are so frequent in our language and children's writing, such as 'to', 'too' and 'two', or 'write', 'right' and 'rite', we can afford to pay them some attention and help students correct errors. We can commit most common homophones to memory, without worrying that they will unravel the confidence of our young brethren (see the table below).

| Common homophones | Common homographs |
|---|---|
| Too/to/two | **Address** |
| Their/there/they're | (n.) where one lives (v.) give |
| Witch/which | a speech |
| Effect/affect | **Date** |
| Weather/whether | (n.) fruit/a calendar time (v.) |
| Break/brake | determine age/go out |
| Your/you're | **Content** |
| By/buy | (adj.) satisfied/happy (n.) |
| Are/our | contained inside something |
| New/knew | **Entrance** |
| Male/mail | (n.) an entry point (v.) to bewitch |
| No/know | or delight someone |
| Where/wear | **Lead** |
| Through/threw | (n.) a type of metal (v.) to go |
| Aloud/allowed | first, leading followers |
| | **Wave** |
| | (v.) a common hand gesture (n.) |
| | a movement of the sea |
| | **Fast** |
| | (adj.) quick (v.) abstain from |
| | food |

Clearly, homographs lead to a misunderstanding of word meanings, whereas homophones are more likely to cause spelling errors. Deep vocabulary knowledge fixes both, alongside a working knowledge of grammar, but we can also apply simple strategies in the classroom too. David Crystal has noted a simple solution for 'stationary' and 'stationery' – a common homophone spelling error:

> A grammatical reminder here would be a distinction between noun (buying some stationery) and adjective (the traffic was stationary). A semantic reminder would be to connect stationery to envelope, for example, with memory reinforcement coming from the repeated 'e's'.
>
> *Spell it out: The singular story of English spelling,* by David Crystal, p. 282

Of course, the best solution to grasping the nuanced differences between homophones and homographs is a broad and deep vocabulary, but recognising common patterns a child can follow, observe and even avoid is useful knowledge for every teacher and student.

Now that we have established the problems that attend spelling rules, it makes sense to highlight common spelling errors and why they happen. Homophone spelling errors are obvious, so we can look out for those and train our students to do the same. Every child is uniquely different, but some spelling problems are very common. Of course, academic vocabulary, as we have seen, is comprised of longer words, with more word parts and some historical letter combinations that are not instantly sensible to a child. According to the Oxford English Corpus – a collection of over 2 billion words in real-life use – there are some very common misspellings, as shown in the following table (find the full list online[6]):

| Correct spelling | Common misspelling |
|---|---|
| Accommodate, accommodation | Acommodate, accomodate |
| Achieve | Acheive |
| Business | Buisness |
| Calendar | Calender, Calander |
| Colleague | Collegue |
| Definitely | Definately |
| Existence | Existance |
| Forty | Fourty |
| Government | Goverment |
| Interrupt | Interupt |
| Knowledge | Knowlege |
| Possession | Posession, possesion |
| Really | Realy |
| Separate | Seperate |
| Surprise | Suprise |
| Tomorrow | Tommorrow, tomorow |
| Truly | Truely |
| Until | Untill |
| Which | Wich |

With some scrutiny of our children's writing we can quickly diagnose their spelling error patterns. When you scan the general misspellings common to us all, some patterns emerge:

- **Double letter errors** are common, e.g. accommodate/ accomodate, interrupt/interupt and tomorrow/tomorow.
- **Phonetic spelling errors** are common, e.g. business/ buisness, calendar/calender and definitely/definately.
- **Omission errors** are common, e.g. double letter omission – really/realy; phonetic spelling omission – which/ wich; general omission.

- **Vowel cluster errors** are common, e.g. homophones like real/reel; long vowels errors like bead/beed; or simply lots of vowels like the word 'queue'.
- **Inflection errors** are common, e.g. loving/loveing, dying/dieing and fatter/fater.

There are individual anomalies like 'yacht' or 'rhythm', or 'soul' and 'bowl', that may simply require deliberate practice, but for most spellings, there is a pattern. Spelling tests can give the illusion that children are learning, as we do improve spelling cumulatively, simply by reading and writing over time, but the reality may be different. In fact, if the reasoning and habits behind spelling mistakes and misconceptions are not fixed, then practice will likely not make perfect. Conversely, such practice may make permanent flaws in our children's spelling and writing.

Too often, teachers are burdened by marking policies that see them correcting or marking for every spelling error. When you have to spend all of your time marking errors, there is little time left for planning to address the underlying issues. We need to reduce how much time teachers spend marking errors in books and increase the time spent on teaching words, their meaning and related spelling patterns.

## Towards a spelling strategy

Need I say more about the need for more than just weekly spelling tests?

When we focus on explicitly teaching the alphabetic code, the etymology and morphology of words, studying and being aware of inflections, whilst addressing common errors with meaningful solutions, then we move towards a successful strategy. '*Look-cover-write-check*' can help to a degree, but it shouldn't be the only tool for a child to learn to spell more credibly.

There are long-standing spelling strategies that are commonly deployed in schools. **Spelling mnemonics** (necessary – one collar, two sleeves) are a handy memory aid. **Finding words within words** is another interesting idea (parliament – I AM parliament). Crucially, however, both of these strategies cannot be used very consistently and therefore they are simply not practical to be used to teach spelling at scale.

Rather than simply enacting weekly spelling texts and relying on mere repetition, we can instead plan to deliberately teach common word roots and patterns in a meaningful structure.

We must then organise our spelling strategey around some core word knowledge that can be used broadly and systematically (see Figure 6.1).

The Department for Education has shared useful guidance on the key components of a balanced spelling programme in their 'Support for Spelling'[7] guide:

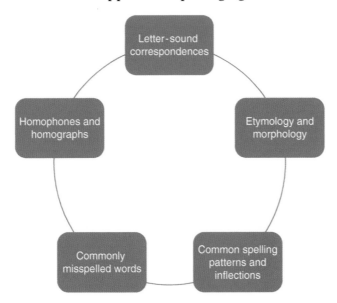

*Figure 6.1*   A vocabulary knowledge-based spelling strategy

A balanced spelling programme includes 5 main components:

a Understanding the principles underpinning word construction (phonemic, morphemic and etymological);
b Recognising how (and how far) these principles apply to each word, in order to learn to spell words;
c Practising and assessing spelling;
d Applying spelling strategies and proof reading;
e Building pupils' self-image as spellers.

*The national strategies primary: Support for spelling,* by Department for Education, 2009, p. 2

The final point – (e) Building pupils' self-image as spellers – is an interesting one. This chapter began with Thomas Jefferson gently chiding his daughter to improve her spelling. Now, any parent or teacher knows the limitations of the 'just tell 'em it is important' approach. This is especially true of teenagers if they detect they are being patronised in any way. We can better build our student's confidence in their spelling if we arm them with the knowledge and strategies to spell better, rather than just test them repeatedly.

The matter of motivation is important because a great deal of accurate spelling comes down to effortful thinking and the tricky, will-sapping act of proofreading, checking and being self-disciplined. For most children, their dominant mode of written communication will be between friends, so the academic code of school and spelling accuracy simply doesn't apply with the same degree of value. Indeed, children can find ingenious spelling alternatives to make themselves appreciated by their peers and separate from their parents and teachers.

We need to give these competing motivations respect, whilst helping children recognise the value and importance of being able to switch from their personal written code between friends, to the academic code of school and the wider world. Andrew Jackson would approve of the creative spellings of our children, but they need to know when to exercise that linguistic dexterity!

We should ask ourselves how we will create a culture within our classroom where the academic code, spelling accuracy and a breadth of vocabulary is used and celebrated? Children will ask 'why' and we need to empower them with that knowledge.

More broadly, in our classrooms, departments and schools, we need to air out our attitudes towards spelling (it may include uncomfortable revelations about our own spelling issues), before agreeing upon a coherent and cumulative strategy towards teaching vocabulary and the accurate spelling of those words. This is rich and powerful knowledge that should sit at the heart of our curriculum and in every classroom.

## IN SHORT...

- Issuing a weekly spelling test is not *teaching* spelling. I repeat, testing is not teaching.
- The teaching of spelling can and should be supported by language origins: etymology and morphology. The explicit teaching of vocabulary offers a prime opportunity to teach and consolidate spelling knowledge.
- The Latin and Greek origins of our academic language offer fertile ground to pursue common spelling patterns and word meanings.
- Most spelling rules have many infractions meaning they are problematic to teach. We should instead focus on developing children's knowledge of the alphabetic code, alongside common morphological

patterns and grammatical inflections, which are guideposts for spelling decisions.

- There are around 500 homophones in the English language. We need to ensure that we highlight these anomalies so that children don't make all-too-common errors. In fact, the 500 or so spelling patterns in the English language, rather than dismissed as chaotic and too difficult, can be better learned and understood.
- We must seek out **'what'** misspellings our children are actually exhibiting, understand **'why'** this may be happening, before supporting them with the means to reason **'how'** to spell correctly.

## Notes

1   Moats, L. C. (2005). 'How spelling supports reading: And why is more regular and predictable than you might think'. *The American Educator*, Winter 2005/2006. Accessed online on 7 May 2014 at: www.aft.org/sites/default/files/periodicals/Moats.pdf.

2   Alderman, G. L., & Green, S. K. (2011). 'Fostering lifelong spellers through meaningful experiences'. *The Reading Teacher*, 64: 599–605. doi:10.1598/RT.64.8.5.

3   Winch, G., Johnston, R. R., March, P., Ljungdahl, L., & Holliday, M. (2010). *Literacy: Reading, writing and children's literature* (4th ed.). South Melbourne: Oxford University Press.

4   Ibid.

5   This phonemic chart is adapted from The British Council pronunciation chart. Accessed online on 6 March 2017 at: www.teachingenglish.org.uk/article/phonemic-chart.

6   Oxford Dictionaries (2017). 'Common misspellings'. Oxford: Oxford University Press. Accessed online on 12 June 2017 at: https://en.oxforddictionaries.com/spelling/common-misspellings.

7  Department for Education (2009). *The National strategies: Primary: 'Support for spelling'* (2nd ed.). Accessible online on 14 December 2017 at: http://webarchive.nationalarchives.gov. uk/20110813013929/http://teachingandlearningresources. org.uk/collection/35326.

# 7 Practical strategies for closing the vocabulary gap

How do you teach a new word?

Every teacher has taught new words on countless occasions, but how many teachers could articulate a method? We should question why we cannot refine and define how we teach new words when the benefits of helping children to grow their vocabulary is so obvious.

For too long in my teaching career I muddled along. My habitual response to a child seeking out the meaning of a new, unfamiliar word would be to encourage them to 'grab a dictionary'. Every desk in my classroom is populated with a dictionary to encourage an independent approach to word learning. On many occasions, a quick check would suffice. So, what is the problem? Well, perhaps unsurprisingly, given prior knowledge and our existing vocabulary is so vital to learning new words, how well a child uses a dictionary relates to their existing word-hoard.

The traditional use of the dictionary is found wanting and they can actually worsen vocabulary gaps in our classrooms if we don't pay close attention to their use. First, dictionary definitions are found to be inaccessible to most students, particularly children with a restricted vocabulary.[1] Given many academic words have multiple meanings – they are *polysemous* – you need to know a lot about a word to select the right meaning. Take just a couple of common words encountered in the school day that have multiple meanings that could be misinterpreted:

**Harmony** is used in music to denote musical notes played simultaneously, but in common use, *harmony* describes a general state of positive agreement. So, *harmony* could be used by a child to describe music, but we could just as easily see *harmony* used in a drama lesson to describe the behaviour of characters.

**Cracking** can be used in everyday speech to describe something as impressive. A common idiom is to describe someone as '*cracking* under pressure' (never mind a 'crack down', or 'cracking the whip'). The most likely dictionary definition of *cracking* is to 'break into parts, or begin to separate'. Finally, in chemistry, *cracking* represents the process whereby complex organic hydrocarbons are broken down into simpler molecules.

Picking up the dictionary in the chemistry classroom is clearly problematic. It can prove a general problem for word learning in schools. Put simply, dictionaries were not designed with novice readers in mind. They are practically limited by space, and so concise, dense definitions are the norm. Even in school-friendly dictionaries, the issues that come with polysemous words are not always overcome. For obvious reasons, 'student friendly examples' are recommended when teaching a word instead of traditional dictionary definitions. Given a child needs around 95% word knowledge, for a typical page from a school textbook – around 300 words – they may struggle with up to 15 words, then deciding upon the most effective strategy to fill in word knowledge gaps is important.

My second most common course of action for a child struggling to grasp a new word would be a brief explanation, or recommending that they 'look back at the sentence and look out for clues around the word'. Once more, this strategy has often proved successful enough. Well, just good enough for me to not notice whether they have *really* understood the word or not. In Isabel Beck and colleagues' brilliant *Bringing Words to Life*, they exemplify how working out the meaning of words from context clues is deeply problematic (this is especially true for students with a limited vocabulary). They define four different types of contexts related to a new or unknown word:

- **Misdirective contexts**: contexts that are unhelpful and lead children towards an incorrect meaning, e.g. the prince was tall, strong and **petrified**.
  [Here the child is expecting the word to mean something related to strong and powerful, whereas the writer has playfully reversed this expectation.]
- **Non-directive contexts**: contexts that offer little help to children, e.g. the prince was **abject**.
  [Here there is simply not enough information to infer any meaning of this complex word from the context.]
- **General contexts**: contexts with surrounding descriptions or information to make confident guesses as to the correct meaning of the word, e.g. at every ball, the prince bored the partygoers with his **obtuse** character and dull conversations.
  [Here there is enough to infer that the word means the prince is dull and boring, but it doesn't characterise all aspects of the word. An added problem with this general meaning is that the word 'obtuse' also describes angles in maths, making it ripe for misinterpretation.]
- **Directive contexts**: contexts with surrounding descriptions or definition information to make precise meanings

clear, e.g. an **obtuse angle** is an angle between 90 and 180 degrees.
[Here the meaning is precise and exact with little room for confusion.]

In many textbooks, the writers have made careful attempts at creating directive contexts, as well as adding glossaries, key words and images to support understanding. Despite such efforts, children encounter many texts daily that offer new, challenging words, but with little contextual support to independently understand those words. In short, don't rely on children to use a dictionary successfully, nor guess from the context of a sentence or a text. Independent word learning is vital, but sometimes children simply lack the requisite knowledge, so explicit vocabulary teaching is required to support word learning.

Let's then define a method for such explicit vocabulary teaching. Teaching individual words (and related words) can be adaptable, but each teacher will likely move through the following phases[2] of the **SEEC model** (see Figure 7.1) to ensure children develop the necessary understanding of important words.

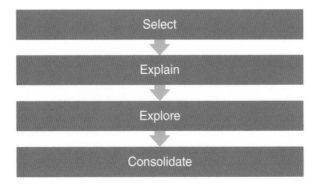

*Figure 7.1*　The SEEC model

## Select

Preview the reading material for the lesson, or the topic or scheme of learning at hand, and then determine the following:

- How difficult is this reading material to understand?
- What words are most important to understand the text or topic?
- What words are unlikely to be part of a child's prior knowledge?
- What words lack helpful, directive contexts?
- What words appear repeatedly in a text and a topic?
- What words are interrelated and help children know additional words?
- What words are frequently encountered in many subject disciplines (Tier 2 words)?

## Explain

Once you have selected the words to teach (of course, words can be taught spontaneously as they arise in classroom talk, etc.), we then move onto explaining the word successfully with this process:

- Say the word carefully (remember the importance of 'phonemic awareness').
- Write the word (this offers opportunities to reference common sounds or letters in the word).
- Give a student friendly definition, for example, *obtuse* – not very sensitive or slow to understand.
- Give multiple meaningful examples, for example, the prince was being deliberately obtuse.
- Ask for student examples and clarify multiple meanings or any misconceptions.

## Explore

Further exploration of a new word isn't *always* essential, nor is it always practical, but it should be a consideration for important words that are integral to understanding. The options are endless and the rest of the chapter supports ideas for exploring words and their meaning. Here are some optional methods to explore the meaning of a word, prompting that all important 'word depth' and evoking 'word consciousness':

- Explore the etymology and common word parts to explore meaning.
- Explore any common word families, interesting synonyms or antonyms for the word/s.
- Explore how the word may be used differently in different disciplines.
- Explore multiple-choice questions that offer examples of the word in use.
- Explore understanding of the word with peers in 'think-pair-share' fashion.
- Explore understanding with children restating the meaning of the word/s in their own words.
- Explore further questions prompted by the word.
- Explore more examples of the word in use.
- Explore related images or ideas evoked by the word.
- Explore strategies to remember the word or concept, e.g. mnemonics.

To give an example, we could explore the word 'obtuse' in many ways. The etymology reveals the word comes from the Latin 'obtusus', meaning 'blunt or dull'. We see the prefix 'ob', meaning 'in front of; against' – seen in words like 'object', 'obsession' and 'obdurate'. You can explore the related meaning in describing a rounded (blunt) leaf, or its meaning in relation to geometry, where an 'obtuse angle' is one that is not so sharp – linking back to the notion of blunt. Students could discuss in pairs and write sentences describing obtuse characters in English, or historical figures in history. They could create their own dictionary definition for their peers, or think of an image or symbol to help remember the word.

## Consolidate

We know that to deeply understand a word we need to repeatedly be exposed to that word. Also, we need to allow for a little forgetting, before retrieving the word again, thereby strengthening how well we remember the word. If we can make the word meaningful by getting children to extend its use outside of the classroom, then all the better. Here are some ways we can consolidate word knowledge over time:

- **Test and learn**. There are words that can be known by students quickly (remember 'fast mapping') and without much explicit focus. Typically though, a child needs to encounter a new academic word multiple times to know that word with some depth of understanding. From our initial explanations and discussion of a word, we may use examples, ask questions and recap what our children know in a given lesson. It is then important to revisit the word, or words, after time has passed, to ensure the word has been embedded properly in long-term memory. 'Cumulative quizzing' and 'short-answer questions' are common testing methods that allow for repeat exposures to words.
- **Using the word in the world**. Too much of what our children learn is seldom repeated in the wider world. With vocabulary, we are offered the opportunity to

use interesting new words in real contexts. Every child has experienced the flush of pride when they have used a new word at home that has impressed their audience. Given the usefulness of many academic words (particularly those '*Tier 2*' words), children can use these terms in their talk and writing in all kinds of scenarios. Encouraging, nurturing and modelling this '*way with words*' can help children become more confident.

- **Research and record.** Many a research activity in school has been lost to a stealthy YouTube search, or a well-meaning jaunt through endless pointless websites. With targeted research, we can guide students to finding out more about words – their histories, families and complex meanings – whilst developing their capacity to learn more words independently. Obviously, a good quality Internet search is dependent upon good quality word knowledge and the right key word selections. Many schools deploy vocabulary books or similar, so that children can visibly grow their vocabulary and make a meaningful record of their learning.

Try it for yourself. Take an upcoming lesson, a topic, or a potential sequence of lessons, and use the **SEEC model** to plan for deliberate, explicit vocabulary development. Some words will need in-depth *exploration*, whereas others will require *explaining* and future *consolidation*.

If we begin to consider vocabulary learning not as a one-off, but as developed over time, we think more about not just words of the day, but a full consideration of word learning daily, weekly, monthly and annually. Considering your teaching with vocabulary in mind in this way can unlock your 'word consciousness', prompting you to generate lots of useful learning opportunities you may not have devised before.

## Developing 'word rich classrooms'

So what does great teaching of vocabulary look like and how do we create 'word rich classrooms'? There are no decisive answers or evidence in this regard, but this offers us countless opportunities to innovate, evaluate and learn about how we best develop the word-hoard of the children in our schools.

Our long-standing experience shows that if we are solely reliant on simply testing word lists, or wielding shiny glossaries that disappear to the back of children's books, never to be seen again, then word learning will be stunted and stultifying. This limited approach to vocabulary teaching and learning, armed with a dictionary and a few tests, in the hope that some learning sticks, needn't be how we go about fostering 'word consciousness'. Instead, we can foster a potent curiosity for words that makes learning infectious and inspiring, making children think harder than they may have thought possible about words.

We know that the most reliable method to broaden and deepen the vocabulary of children in our schools is to get them **reading** a significant amount (remember, a good reader can read a million words a year or more). We know that we need to immerse children in classrooms that are rich with vocabulary and **academic talk**. We know that words are related and connected, most often organised into categories, and that we best learn when we foster making **connections and categorising**. We know a greater understanding of word depth can be spurred by skilful **word play**.

These four strands (shown in Figure 7.2) then offer us a method for creating our own word rich classrooms, adapting and applying these general methods to the different disciplines within our school curriculum.

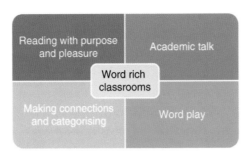

*Figure 7.2* 'Word rich' classrooms

## Reading with purpose and pleasure … to close the vocabulary gap

The case for children reading widely and deeply is incontrovertible. You would struggle to find a teacher who does not, or would not, recommend reading for pleasure (if you do, tell them they are wrong). We know that once children begin reading with some fluency that most new words are learned from reading and not from being taught explicitly.[3] A good reader can read around a million words a year, being exposed to something like 20,000 to 40,000 new words.[4] It is a pleasure that proves immensely valuable to children in many ways.

Crucially though, simply encouraging wider reading, or dressing up once a year to herald a 'reading day', won't close the vocabulary gaps in our classrooms. As you would expect, good readers enjoy reading more than weak readers. The early reading gap widens and hardens into academic failure. We should aim then for a systematic approach to fostering a culture of reading with effectiveness *and* reading for pleasure. Read well and children can begin to read with pleasure.

Developing any sort of culture in a school requires planning, preparation and time. The following strategies, when combined intelligently to suit our school context, could develop a positive culture for reading:

- **Make it easy, attractive, social and timely (the EAST framework).** The 'Behavioural Insights Team' – more commonly known as the '*nudge unit*', utilise behavioural science to show how we can shift habits and create positive cultures within groups of people. In schools, for teachers, children and parents, reading needs to be easy. For children, this can mean easy access to interesting books; for parents, it means providing books and apt reading lists; whereas for teachers it could mean better training on teaching reading. To make reading a daily norm and attractive, we need well-resourced reading environments. To make it social and timely, we can use technology to communicate to parents (text messaging has proven an effective method to reach parents[5]), whilst finding explicit times in the school week where reading can be enshrined.

- **Reading role models.** We know that one of the most powerful influences on children is their friends and peers. Harnessing this truth positively could include strategies like '**peer reading**', seeing older children matched with younger children, or within groups, stronger readers matched with their less confident peers. At home, programmes that involve parents, like the **FRED** (Father's Reading Every Day) programme, supports fathers to read with their children,[6] offering important reading role models.

- **'Living libraries'.** The last decade has seen a sad decline in local libraries. This makes the importance of our school libraries even more pronounced. A healthy, well-used library is a strong indicator of the reading culture of a school. Schools that invest in making libraries a well-used resource utilise technology (searching the web should go hand in hand with traditional book searches), and see school systems like homework clubs or 'prep' being integrated into the school library use.

- 'The million word challenge!' Sometimes we need a little motivation. We can initiate a reading challenge that encourages the reading of books *and* conveys the crucial message of how important it is for children to possess a wealth of words. This message getting to parents is vital, as parents understanding the vocabulary gap can prove a step towards recruiting their support. Many other reading challenges fit the bill. Schools like Wellington Academy have a '*40 Book Challenge*' to encourage the habit of regular reading on a weekly basis.

- Stopping the 'Summer Slide'. It is an annual problem that children forget what they have learnt given the weeks on holiday during the summer. Unfortunately, children who have few books at home, often wedded to a word-poor environment, can fall behind further than their peers. By targeting book loans and free books, setting reading challenges or by offering targeted 'summer schools' or similar supports, we can halt the slide.

- Seek out expert support. Organisations like The Literacy Trust do a fantastic job of supporting schools to develop a reading culture.

We need to ensure that we have a culture of thriving reading, but this needs to be balanced with high quality reading instruction and an emphasis on vocabulary development in the classroom. If we are planning with vocabulary in mind, or pre-teaching important vocabulary, then explicit strategies can help bolster our efforts. We can foster word-rich classrooms by undertaking some of the following classroom-based strategies:

- Recording 'keystone' words. There are many examples of children recording and charting their vocabulary development, whether it is in 'word records' or 'word-hoards' and so on. By foregrounding academic language

147

in this way, we offer a method to make explicit the value of new, interesting words.

- **Word walls**. We can help create an accessible, word rich environment by including vocabulary on classroom walls. The obvious issue here is having walls laden with vocabulary that becomes little more than wallpaper. By including student friendly definitions and examples, we can make such word walls useful, integrating them into our daily practice more strategically.

- **Knowledge organisers with word glosses**. A common approach to supporting children's reading and under-standing are knowledge organisers. They provide a con-cise summary of a topic or text on a side of A4. They can prove particularly useful as a glossary of 'keystone' vocabulary to support learning and offer a quick and easy reference tool.

- **Read alouds**. Too often, we assume that a session of reading aloud to groups is only for young children. We should instead consider read alouds for every class-room, as it allows us to read complex texts that children would normally struggle to read independently, whilst surrounding such reading with rich talk. Our fluent speech and instantaneous decoding can help children focus on the meaning of unfamiliar and challenging vocabulary, particularly in elaborate academic sentence structures (a strategy so crucial given the increased reading demands of the new curriculum).

- **Reciprocal reading**. One method for reading collabo-ratively in small groups is 'reciprocal reading'. Given the collective word-hoards of children can typically outmatch any individual, we offer the opportunity for children to discuss word meanings in a more structured fashion. This method includes assigning roles: the '*sum-mariser*', '*questioner*', '*clarifier*' and '*predictor*', which makes explicit the strategies deployed by good readers.

- **Writing to consolidate reading**. We know that taking notes and summarising a given text is a well-established strategy to support children's comprehension of what they read. And yet, too often, we can expect children to make well-organised, sophisticated notes without training children how to do so. Models like '**Triplicate note-making**', comprised of three columns (Column 1 – core information; Column 2 – key questions; Column 3 – memorable words, images and mnemonics), offers a way to best summarise the understanding of a given text.

- **Dictionary training**. We know that children can struggle with dictionaries, but specific dictionaries designed for use by children can make the process of searching out meanings much more successful. For example, the **Collins COBUILD dictionary**, based on how words are used frequently, is good for practical use. Visual dictionaries and bilingual dictionaries are helpful for novice word learning. Also, websites like '**One Look Dictionary**' (www.onelook.com), the dictionary of online dictionaries, and '**Vocabulary.com**' (www.vocabulary.com), which has a wealth of excellent lists on morphology and word roots (www.vocabulary.com/lists/morphology-and-roots/) offer us a tool to use with some appropriate training.

## Academic talk … to close the vocabulary gap

Just as developing a reading culture requires nurturing, with systematic planning and a shared sense of purpose, so does creating a culture of academic talk. Growing a culture of rich academic talk begins with children and teachers understanding the nuances of academic talk and how words and phrases are crafted and adapted, and how special codes of communication are built and broken.

We begin with teacher talk. Alongside reading, teacher talk and explanations are the source of much of the complex academic vocabulary our children learn on a daily basis.[7] Too often, though, explanations and teacher talk are taken for granted. Rather curiously, we have even seen teacher talk derided in some quarters, with the implicit assumption that children talking is the font of all knowledge and understanding. It is an unfortunate case of putting the cart before the horse.

To develop a strong culture that values academic talk, we should then begin with practical strategies that focus on high-quality teacher talk that elicits sophisticated talk from children:

- **Model the code.** We know that talk lacks the rare academic vocabulary and complex structures of what we read, so our modelling of using academic talk is key. We may emphasise the slightly bookish use of discourse markers, stressing such words for emphasis in our talk. For example, in art, you may explain differences in painterly style in this way: 'The abstract work of Picasso **is in stark contrast** to the realism and formal balance of Manet. **Nevertheless**, both artists share ...'. The language can feel elaborate and unnatural at first, but with practice, it can become a habit of our explanations. By using the **SEEC model** (*select, explain, explore* and *consolidate*) we can confidently increase the complexity of the vocabulary we use in our explanations and teacher talk.
- 'Talk like an expert'. As we model academic talk and sophisticated vocabulary choices, we need to make this implicit code explicit to children. In each subject discipline, we should make explicit how an expert speaks. So to speak like a scientist, we may have to define the *Tier 3* and *Tier 2* language deployed by a scientist and focus on how a scientist uses logic, reason and supporting

evidence. Questions like 'can you explain your thinking with evidence?' can probe a student's thinking, followed up with 'how would you test your hypothesis?' or 'how confident are you in your thinking?' By probing degrees of confidence in science, we reveal how a scientist thinks in probabilities rather than certainties. Conditional words like 'likely', 'unlikely', 'probably' 'presumably', 'may' and 'suggests' are helpful to support scientific talk and thinking.

- **Signposting synonyms.** Children constantly respond to teacher talk with language that is comprehensible, but not precise or academic in style. Constantly raising the bar of their vocabulary use can become habitual with practice, seeing children implicitly take on using academic vocabulary in their talk. Little verbal prompts can nudge everyday vocabulary upwards with academic synonyms. For example, in physical education, 'tired muscles' becomes 'muscle **fatigue**'; or in science, 'my idea ...' is nudged with a teacher reply of 'my **hypothesis** ...', with 'the body gets rid of ...' becoming 'the body **excretes** ...'. We needn't correct children; we can simply restate with the new academic words in use.

- **'What about wait time?'** We have known for decades that there is a fundamental flaw in teacher talk. We offer children too little time to think when we ask a question.[8] By giving children little over a second to answer a question, we limit the likelihood of children offering extended responses with academic vocabulary. If we are going to ask hard questions, then we need to provide the basic support factor of time.

- **The power of 'why'.** We know that it is crucial for children to activate their prior knowledge to talk and think through a problem, or to explain a concept. If we are to get children talking like an expert using academic language, we need to ask the right type of question.

By asking more 'why' questions we get children to better trigger their prior knowledge and think harder. In history, it could be simply, 'why is the death of Archduke Franz Ferdinand so significant?', or in food technology, a question like 'why are fats and carbohydrates important to the human body?'[9]

- **ABC feedback.** This simply talk scaffold can have a transformative effect on the talk and dialogue in classrooms. By asking children to **Agree with**, **Build upon** or **Challenge** the responses of their peers, it allows students to develop their ideas in a more disciplined fashion, whilst giving a helpful scaffold to their ideas. By selecting the right children, based on an escalating degree of challenge, you can ensure that talk is in depth and communicated in academic language.

Once we have emphasised and defined high-quality academic teacher talk, alongside dialogue with and between children, we begin to also enhance the quality of children's talk. If we scaffold, guide and support their talk, we get them using academic words and more deeply understanding those words.

- **'Ask, explain'.** Research on word explanations has shown that young children do learn when teachers re-read stories and give additional word explanations.[10] Most interestingly, when children themselves explained their own definitions of the words in question, they made the greatest gains in word learning.
- **Twenty Questions.** We know that children can go hours in school without asking a question[11] and it can have implications for them using and understanding academic vocabulary. Such questioning and hard thinking can be cultivated. By getting children to generate as many questions as they can about an upcoming topic,

we can draw out their prior knowledge and get them thinking about what they know and need to know. The words they use prove revealing about their degrees of knowledge. In English Literature, if *'Twenty Questions'* on **'Romeo and Juliet'** reveals words and concepts like love and marriage, we can quickly probe whether they know and understand 'courtly love' or 'unrequited love'.

- **'Just a Minute'**. This popular radio game offers us a perfectly formed model for encouraging extended academic talk. With rules barring the repetition of words during the minute countdown, we force children to think quickly about what they know 'and encourage the use of appropriate' synonyms where necessary.

- **'Explore and explain'**. This vocabulary challenge sees children working in pairs or small teams to explain 'keystone words' to their peers, who are blindfolded, or simply facing the other way. By using timers and point scoring, you can make this activity a lively approach to revising important words. This highlights to students the vital importance of clarity and the elaborate detail often needed to make a thing, concept or idea understood.

- **'Study group'**. We can draw upon the power of talk when tackling extended reading. By apportioning the reading task in parts, issuing a part each to an individual child, you can encourage children to both read and summarise with a real sense of purpose. You can encourage note making or the highlighting of 'keystone words' where appropriate, with the outcome being a shared knowledge and understanding of the reading at hand.

## Making connections and categorising … to close the vocabulary gap

We know that words are related and are members of meaningful families. When we make a concerted attempt to help children make those connections we encourage 'word consciousness'. There are of course many opportunities offered by word roots and word parts, as this book has made clear, but we can also use other models to connect words together to help children grow their vocabulary.

We can use visual cues, by using '**graphic organisers**', or help children categorise by meaning, similarity and difference. Various 'graphic organisers' can get children thinking in different ways about the words they encounter:

Frayer Diagrams. This type of graphic organiser is really very versatile and adaptable to different subject disciplines. Take a look at the two following examples:

1 **Frayer model – English poetry design**. This model can be used with a crucial word in a given poem that requires in-depth analysis (such as "chartered" in William Blake's poem 'London') (see Figure 7.3).
2 **Frayer model – standard design**. This model could be used in maths, science and countless other subjects to lead children to a deeper understanding of a word (see Figure 7.4).

Venn diagrams. This model offers a commonly used method to both group words but also compare words,

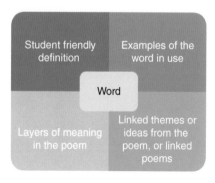

*Figure 7.3*   Frayer model – English poetry design

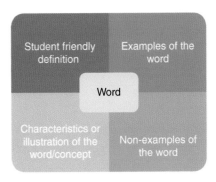

*Figure 7.4*   Frayer model – standard design

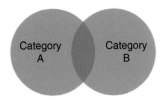

*Figure 7.5*   Venn diagrams

highlighting similarity, difference and overlapping meanings (see Figure 7.5).

**Word maps.** This organiser offers a model to unpick a complex word or concept with multiple related meanings or sub-topics. For example, look at this physics example in Figure 7.6 for the topic of '**forces**'.

Concept maps. A close relation to 'Word maps', concept maps are a hierarchical model for connections and organising key words and ideas that define a concept. An example is shown in Figure 7.7.

There are many variations on the theme of grouping and categorising words. Children with a wealth of words can seemingly do this 'naturally', but for children with a restricted academic vocabulary, it can prove more of a challenge that requires support and modelling. Here are some strategies that help children connect words, vary

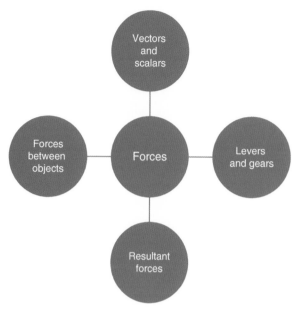

*Figure 7.6*   Word maps

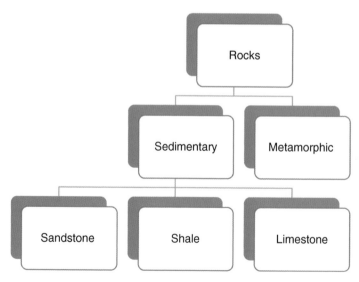

*Figure 7.7*   Concept maps

their word choices or make more considered word choices in their own talk or writing:

- **'Word scales'.** Give children a group of related words by topic or theme, for example, measurement in science, shapes in maths, or eras in history. Children have to take the group of *Tier 3* words and categorise them as they see fit, such as the number of sides for the mathematical shapes, or scaled chronologically for historical eras.
- **'Word ladder'.** With narrative writing in English, or a discipline with extended writing, you could enhance students' vocabulary by encouraging students to up the quality of their word choices. If they use 'ugly', we can take steps up the word ladder with 'unsightly', 'hideous', 'grotesque' or 'repugnant'. In an academic essay, 'got better' becomes 'improved', 'enhanced' or 'ameliorated'. Such ladders can be made visible on 'word walls' in classrooms.
- **'Meaning lines'.** Choose a familiar word pairing, such as 'walk' and 'run', and then get students to create a line between the two. On this line they have to create a sequence of words that convey shades of meaning from 'walk' to 'run', for example, 'prance', 'meander', 'stroll', 'lope', 'jog', 'dart' and 'sprint'. Try it yourself with an emotion meaning line, from 'happy' to 'sad'.
- **Flashcards.** A common word learning tool and revision strategy, flashcards are another active way to both organise and categorise words and their meanings. Remember though, students need training to devise good flashcards.
- **'Word pairs'.** Useful for pretty much every subject discipline, you can pair up real and fake words to tease out their prior knowledge. With some clever play with familiar prefixes and so on, you can catch out a lot of children who are overconfident in their vocabulary knowledge.

- 'Word triplets'. Give children three synonyms and they can choose between them to identify the most effective/ least effective/out one out. Take these examples here and consider the subtle judgments of effectiveness or the exceptions:

| | | |
|---|---|---|
| Honour | Old | Modern |
| Privilege | Ancient | New-fangled |
| Nobility | Debilitated | Contemporary |

- **Prefix/suffix matching**. You can make visible to students the word building that is so essential to academic vocabulary and to growing vocabulary.

| | |
|---|---|
| Un | Circular |
| Re | Likely |
| Dis | Play |
| Semi | Matter |
| Anti | Embody |

## Word play ... to close the vocabulary gap

Learning new words shouldn't ever prove a dull, work-a-day activity. Words are intriguing and revealing. Words are flexible, silly, secretive, surprising, sophisticated and even playful. Given this excellent material, we should bring the power of word play into the classroom.

A good place to start is by recognising how **figurative language** (words or phrases with a meaning beyond the literal), language play and vocabulary curiosities are all around us:

- **Pseudonyms**: a fictitious name, especially used by authors, for example, George Orwell and Mark Twain.

- **Eponyms**: a person after whom a discovery or place is thought to be named, for example, 'leotard', named after Jules Leotard, or 'sandwich' after the Earl of Sandwich.

- **Toponyms**: a place name; a name derived from an origin or place, for example, 'badminton' after Badminton in Gloucestershire, or 'bikini' after Bikini Atoll.

- **Demonyms**: the name for the people or inhabitants of a place, for example, 'Belgians' for the people of Belgium, or the 'Bhutanese' for the people of Bhutan.

- **Idioms**: a characteristic expression or phrase, for example, 'add insult to injury', or 'barking up the wrong tree'.

- **Proverbs**: a short, well-known saying stating a general truth, for example, 'the pen is mightier than the sword', or 'too many cooks spoil the broth'.

- **Catchphrases**: a short phrase or expression recognised by its repeated use, for example, "Am I bovvered?" – Catherine Tate or "I have a cunning plan" – Baldrick.

- **Slogans**: a memorable motto or phrase used to political or commercial adverts for promotion, for example, "Just do it" – Nike or "Education, education, education" – Tony Blair.

- **Similes**: a figure of speech comparing one thing or another using 'like' or 'as', for example, 'she was as busy as a bee' or 'it was as light as a feather'.

- **Metaphors**: a figure of speech directly comparing one thing to another, for example, 'love is a battlefield' or 'he was an ogre'.

- **Euphemisms**: a figure of speech where a mild or indirect word or expression is used in place of a blunt or harsh expression, for example, 'the dog passed away' or 'the television fell off the back of a truck'.

- **Oxymorons**: a figure of speech where two seemingly contradictory words are used together for effect, for example, 'deafening silence' or 'sweet sorrow'.

- **Collocations**: the habitual use of a word with another word or words, for example, 'academic discipline' or 'artificial intelligence'.
- **Anagrams**: word play where letters in a word or phrase are rearranged to make a new word or expression, for example, 'a gentle man' – 'elegant man' or 'Election results' – 'Lies – let's recount!'
- **Palindromes**: a word or phrase whose sequence of letters reads the same backwards or forwards, for example, 'madam' or 'racecar'.
- **Portmanteaux**: words formed by merging parts of one word to another, for example, 'smog' = smoke and fog.

We can foreground a curiosity for words in many creative ways:

- **'Word of the week'**. This popular strategy establishes a structure to emphasise the rich meanings and stories that attend words.
- **'Word detectives' or 'Word wizards'**. There are various models for encouraging children to seek out, recognise and collect interesting words in use, digging into their etymology and much more.
- **Spelling Bee or 'Spelling Spies'**. The *'Spelling Bee'*, popularised in America, is a lively way to celebrate and explore the varied spellings in our language. Rather than stilted weekly tests, they can offer a fun challenge element to spelling. Similarly, *'Spelling Spies'* encourages children to seek out spelling patterns, with children being given responsibility in class and beyond to take on the mantle of the expert, or to ask interesting questions about spelling.
- **Jokes and puns**. Children, indeed adults, are forever seeking out jokes and puns. My young son Noah is immensely proud of his jokes and his 'developing'

(a definite euphemism) word play. I am not sure his joke, "Question: What is the favourite drink of a whisk? Answer: Whiskey" will stand the test of time like a fine malt, but his creative exploration of words is something I hope he retains.

- **Word coinage.** Given patterns of roots, prefixes and suffixes, children can create words, break words and become word aware in ways that become very useful when encountering new and unfamiliar vocabulary. Why doesn't the word 'defrostise' exist, or 'dispeech'? These questions can really get children thinking.
- **Online word play.** Websites like '**Freerice.com**' tests children on their word knowledge whilst donating rice for charity. '**A.Word.A.Day**' (wordsmith.org/awad) offers what is says on the tin and the **Oxford English Dictionary** and **Merriam-Webster** offer similar handy resources.

## Some final questions

Rather than the usual summary, this chapter ends with some questions about how and why we will go about teaching and learning with vocabulary in mind.

- What practical strategies are appropriate for your classroom and/or your school?
- What practical strategies are most appropriate to specific subject disciplines, or need to be adapted in light of disciplinary specific thinking, speaking, reading and writing?
- If you try one or more of these practical strategies, how will you know they have worked?
- If you try one or more of these practical strategies, what will you stop doing?

Teachers are seldom at a loss for new ideas or new school-wide initiatives. We do need to think hard though about the 'why' and 'how best' of our practice, not just the 'what' of the strategies. For school leaders, questions about supporting teachers with training, tools and time are obvious and important.

## Notes

1  Scott, J. A., & Nagy. W. E. (1997). 'Understanding the definitions of unfamiliar verbs'. *Reading Research Quarterly*, 32 (2): 184–200.

2  There are helpful models and acronyms similar to the model I have proposed, with differences at the level of word preference, such as the STAR method: select, teach, activate and revisit. Blachowicz, C., & Fisher, P. (2005). *Teaching vocabulary in all classrooms* (3rd ed.). New York, NY: Pearson Education.

3  Cunningham, A. E. (2005). 'Vocabulary growth through independent reading and reading aloud to children'. In E. H. Hiebert & M. L. Kamhi (eds.), *Teaching and learning vocabulary: Bringing research to practice* (pp. 45–68). Mahwah, NJ: Lawrence Erlbaum Associates.

4  Grabe, W. (2009). *Reading in a second language: Moving from theory to practice.* New York, NY: Cambridge University Press.

5  Education Endowment Foundation (14 July 2016). 'Texting parents about tests and homework can improve maths results and reduce absenteeism'. Accessed online on 10 August 2017 at: https://educationendowmentfoundation.org.uk/news/texting-parents-about-tests-and-homework-can-improve-maths-results-and-redu/.

6  You can find out more about FRED here: www.fatherhood-institute.org/training-and-consultancy/fathers-reading-day-training/.

7  Biemiller, A. (2012). 'Teaching vocabulary in the primary grades: Vocabulary instruction needed'. In E. J. Kame'enui & J. F. Baumann (eds.), *Vocabulary instruction: Research to practice* (2nd ed.) (pp. 34–50). New York, NY: Guilford Press.

8  Rowe, M. B. (1987). 'Wait time: Slowing down may be a way of speeding up'. *American Educator*, 11 (Spring): 38–43, 47. EJ 351 827.

9 Menke, D., & Pressley, M. (1994). 'Elaborative interrogation: Using "why" questions to enhance the learning from text'. *Journal of Reading,* 37 (8): 642–645.

10 Biemiller, A., &. Boote, C. (2006). 'An effective method for building meaning vocabulary in primary grades'. *Journal of Educational Psychology,* 98: 44–62. doi:10.1037/0022-0663. 98.1.44.

11 Graesser, A. C., & Person, N. K. (1994). 'Question asking during tutoring'. *American Education Research Journal,* 31 (1): 104–137.

# 8 | Next steps

Wise words are carried through time as proverbs. In the Bible story of the disciple Peter healing the lame beggar, he says how he cannot give what he does not have. If we translate this wisdom to the job of teaching, we see that we too often face the same issue: 'one cannot teach what one does not know'.[1]

We know that teachers are typically not familiar with teaching academic vocabulary beyond helping children to use strategies like dictionary definitions and relying on the contexts of sentences to illuminate the meaning of unknown words.[2] There is so much more we can do to support teachers.

We do, as teachers, have a duty to know more about how children in our care can better communicate and access the academic curriculum.

Crucially, as teachers, we need high quality training and support to mediate more challenging reading at every key stage. The transparent problem is that even few English teachers have been taught about the complexity of reading and vocabulary development, never mind busy chemistry, PE or maths teachers. I can say that with the humility of an English teacher who is self-taught regarding pretty much all aspects of the reading process and regarding the value of vocabulary. What hope then is there for a physics teacher? Their students are facing the most complex of academic vocabulary, complicated by increased numeracy demands ... oh, and all of the requisite science knowledge crammed into the new curriculum.

Ultimately, I would wish that, upon reading this book, teachers and school leaders ask pertinent questions about their daily practice and curriculum planning. Alas, I do not provide easy answers, but asking good questions would be an important start. Here are some useful prompts to frame some hard thinking about vocabulary and the challenge of a new curriculum:

1 What vocabulary do the children I teach need to know, understand and use to be successful in school and beyond?
2 How challenging are the reading texts that I expect children to read and understand in my lessons?
3 How do we best select what words to teach?
4 How do I best teach the words I have selected to teach?
5 Are there any barriers or misconceptions related to the words that I have selected to teach?
6 What strategies will I deploy to overcome those barriers and to correct misconceptions?
7 How do we best foster a culture of reading in my classroom and/or school?
8 How do we encourage children to become avid readers beyond the classroom?
9 How do we best foster a culture of rich academic talk in our classroom and/or school?
10 How will we know whether children in our classrooms are successfully growing their vocabulary and that our practice is having a positive impact?

Note the important repetition of the word 'we'. If we are to prove successful in closing the vocabulary gaps in our classrooms, helping children to confidently tackle the challenge of the new curriculum, it will prove a collective endeavour.

## How will we know we are having a positive impact in the classroom?

One of the barriers for vocabulary teaching across the curriculum is that there are too few known classroom-friendly assessments that can measure and support vocabulary growth. Spelling test and word list assessments lack the nuance to unpick 'word depth' in a meaningful way.

Deep vocabulary learning is irreversible, irreplaceable and essential to learning and thinking, but as it is so integral to all of schooling and learning beyond the school gates, it proves very difficult to evaluate effectively. Reading comprehension and vocabulary development isn't easily discernible in examination success either, but it is like oxygen: it is there, we depend on it, but we don't notice it and therefore we take it for granted.

Designing, undertaking and evaluating effective vocabulary instruction is a difficult proposition. Despite there being a great of amount of evidence recognising that vocabulary development is crucial for school success, the equivalent basis for the 'how' of developing vocabulary in the classroom is not so robust. We have work to do, but the rewards for our students are simply too significant not to undertake that work.

It is good to start defining word breadth and depth more specifically. As far back as 1942, researchers like Lee Cronbach have been defining word knowledge. His scale for the dimensions of word knowledge is helpful:

1 **Generalisation**: The ability to define the word.

2 **Application**: The ability to apply the word in appropriate situations.

3 **Breadth**: The ability to know and recall different meanings of the word.

4 **Precision**: The ability to recognise exactly in what situations the word does and does not apply.

5 **Availability**: The ability to use the word in our thinking and in our speech.[3]

Using Cronbach's scale, we can develop and use relatively simple vocabulary assessments in our daily practice with little effort. Oral questioning is an obvious quick and powerful way to assess a child's knowledge and understanding of vocabulary and related concepts. In the previous chapter, the *'Frayer model'* and the *'Meaning map'* both offer opportunities for the teacher to evaluate vocabulary knowledge. Rather than seeing an assessment as the sole preserve of national tests, we should recognise the diagnostic value of using such a graphic organiser to test and develop word knowledge.

One strategy I have begun to make an integral element of my teaching is first selecting the integral vocabulary of a given topic or scheme of learning and then assessing my students' prior knowledge of those words. Using Edgar Dale's **'Four stages of word knowledge'** model,[4] you can do a quick and easy assessment:

1 I have never seen the word before and I do not know it. [1 point]

2 I know there is such a word – I can pronounce it – but I do not know its meaning. [2 points]

3 I have some partial knowledge – I recognise it – I could probably use it in my writing. [3 points]

4 I know the word well – I can use it confidently – I know it changes in different contexts. [4 points]

## Next steps

By creating a point scoring system, you can begin to discern your own approximate thresholds for the depth of word knowledge of children in your class and school. You can take it one step further by getting children to use the words in sentences (this extra step is helpful in reducing a natural over-confidence that children often exhibit when faced with new vocabulary in school). The Dale four-stage model can of course be signalled with a quick show of fingers for ease, so it needn't prove a burdensome paper-pushing exercise. Such vocabulary assessments can offer a great pre-teaching activity that primes children to learn a new challenging topic, for example, as shown in the following table.

### Vocabulary knowledge: 'Power and conflict poetry'

| Vocabulary | Never heard of it | Heard of it, but couldn't use it | I might be able to use it | I know it and can use it confidently |
|---|---|---|---|---|
| Antique | | | | |
| Visage | | | | |
| Decay | | | | |
| Pedestal | | | | |
| Total point score: ...... | | | | |

Alternatively, teachers can use Dale's model with a sample of vocabulary from Avril Coxhead's 'Academic Word List' (see Appendix 4) to gain a more general sense of a child's academic vocabulary knowledge. These *Tier 2* words are the words we can teach, but also words that we can assess meaningfully.

We can check word knowledge with mini-assessments that begin to decipher greater word depth, with verbal questions and quick short answer quizzes being available, for example:

1  Have you heard of word X?
2  Does word X have something to do with A, B, C or D?
3  The word X means (A) Definition 1 (B) Definition 2 (C) Definition 3 (D) Definition 4.
4  Do you know any synonyms for X?
5  Do you know any antonyms for X?

Synonym or antonym matching activities can both be a useful way to assess vocabulary knowledge, which also encourages exposure to new words, such as this 'match the synonym' assessment:

| | |
|---|---|
| Tired | Vibrant |
| Dynamic | Tropical |
| Wintry | Despicable |
| Scorching | Lethargic |
| Serious | Frigid |
| Appalling | Grave |

'**Multiple-choice questions**' are a popular and common method of assessment, with child-friendly word definitions being offered for the vocabulary selected. '**Cloze exercises**' are another perennial favourite, with '**short answer quizzes**' proving a mainstay in the teacher's repertoire. '**Flashcards**' offer the opportunity for self-testing vocabulary – with children devising their own or using online tests (e.g. **Quizlet**).

Classroom based strategies are as useful for developing vocabulary knowledge as they are for diagnosing gaps in word knowledge. They can lack information about underlying knowledge about how well children can use those words and so on. To get a more thorough measure of vocabulary knowledge and the related ability of children to fully comprehend a difficult text, there are standardised assessments:

- **Peabody Picture Vocabulary Test, Fourth Edition**. This test measures listening and understanding of single-vocabulary items. It is typically used with younger children and requires substantial input to undertake the test.
- **Single Word Reading Test (SWRT)**. This quick word-reading test offers Standard Age Scores and diagnostic information. It can prove relatively easy to administer.
- **York Assessment of Reading Comprehension (YARC)**. Divided into age-appropriate assessments, the YARC identifies decoding and comprehension skills. The secondary assessment includes a range of fiction and non-fiction extracts. The test is one-to-one, so it is appropriate for more specialist, individual support for children.
- **InCAS**. This primary assessment covers a broad span of reading, spelling, maths and mental arithmetic. The reading element tests word recognition, decoding and comprehension.
- **MidYIS**. The secondary school equivalent test to InCAS, this test specifically assesses vocabulary: word fluency and understanding, as part of the broader academic assessment.
- **New Group Reading Test (NGRT)**. This assessment is made up of two parts. Sentence completion: predominantly measuring decoding, as well as passage comprehension. Weaker readers do a phonics test. This assessment offers Standard Age Scores and detailed diagnostic information.

Selecting these standardised assessments is a significant investment of time and money. If we use them to find a baseline assessment of vocabulary knowledge and reading comprehension, we offer a robust diagnostic assessment from which to evaluate the progress of children in our schools. Such assessments would clearly be embedded in a whole-school assessment model.

The mention of whole-school planning raises a crucial consideration regarding school development. Every teacher can have a significant influence on the success of children in their classroom, but the best schools have a strong leadership at all levels of the school. To create a reading culture and support teachers in tackling the challenges of a new curriculum, senior leadership support is an essential prerequisite. Helping every child crack the academic code needs a strong strategy and the more consistent it is across a school, the more likelihood of success.

## Whole school strategies for closing the vocabulary gap

One pioneering school in London, Greenshaw High School, has undertaken a whole-school approach to vocabulary development, spear-headed by school leader Phil Stock, to develop explicit vocabulary teaching. It offers us a very useful example:

### Case study: Explicit vocabulary teaching at Greenshaw High School

We are now into the third year of our school-wide focus on explicit vocabulary teaching and we are starting to see the impact on student learning. Our strategy has two components – a dedicated programme of roots, prefixes and suffixes, which is taught during tutor time – as well as a whole school approach to teaching *Tier 2* and *Tier 3* vocabulary in the classroom. We trialled both approaches before we implemented them more widely across year groups and subject areas.

In order to provide on-going support and to account for the nuances of different subjects, we appointed language leads from each of the main departments and faculty areas.

## Next steps

Language leads work closely with the language coordinator to develop their understanding of vocabulary teaching and to develop approaches tailored to their specific contexts. They provide support to department colleagues through subject pedagogy training sessions and by developing agreed definitions, resources and strategies to aid classroom delivery.

Tutors in year 7 and 8 receive upfront training on how to deliver the bespoke root programme, with the plan to extend this to older year groups on a year on year basis. The programme aims to develop students' understanding of the most commonly used roots, prefixes and suffixes across the curriculum, which subject teachers can then draw upon in their lessons when teaching subject-specific terminology. Pre- and post-assessment comparisons during the trial phase suggested student's etymological knowledge had improved considerably.

As well as providing extensive training, we have developed additional tools to support vocabulary teaching. Whole school protocols for teaching *Tier 2* and *Tier 3* words, for instance, provide clear reference points for teachers learning how to make direct language teaching a routine feature of their practice. At KS3, school planners have been replaced by language journals. They identify the vocabulary to learn and provide space for students to record definitions in their own words, put new words into example sentences and devise graphical representations to help recall in the future.

Our approach is still very much in its infancy and it will be a while yet before teachers are fully conversant with teaching etymology, meanings, analogies and using graphical representations as part of their daily practice. End of year core vocabulary assessments are one way we measure impact and identify areas for improvement in the future.

Back in Chapter 1, there was a proposed sequence of seven steps to help schools and teachers plan for vocabulary development. You can see how those steps are being undertaken in schools like Greenshaw High School:

1 Train teachers to become more knowledgeable and confident in explicit vocabulary teaching.
2 Teach academic vocabulary explicitly and clearly, with coherent planning throughout the curriculum.
3 Foster structured reading opportunities in a model that supports students with vocabulary deficits.
4 Promote and scaffold high-quality academic talk in the classroom.
5 Promote and scaffold high quality academic writing in the classroom.
6 Foster 'word consciousness' in our students (e.g. sharing the etymology and morphology of words).
7 Teach students independent word learning strategies.

These are steps we can undertake in every school, from small infant schools, to large secondary schools and further education colleges. Of course, in many classrooms and schools, skilled teachers are undertaking some of these steps with success. We need to shine a light on that expertise.

Teachers and school leaders require support factors to help their students grapple with the challenges posed by academic language. Great teachers can make a powerful difference for students, but we need to coordinate our efforts. Remember the 'Peter principle'? You cannot teach what you do not know. Therefore, a programme of continuous professional development, supported by evidence and expertise, is required for us to help *every* teacher to close the vocabulary gap in their classroom.

In the Department for Education 'Standard for Teachers' Professional Development',[5] we find a handy framework upon which to base our professional training:

1  Professional development should have a focus on improving and evaluating pupil outcomes.
2  Professional development should be underpinned by robust evidence and expertise.
3  Professional development should include collaboration and expert challenge.
4  Professional development programmes should be sustained over time.
5  Professional development must be prioritised by school leadership.

Would the professional development in your school fare well when evaluated against this framework? What would a programme for vocabulary development based on this framework look like in your school context? A better professional knowledge and understanding of how vocabulary is an essential thread in the fabric of all teaching and learning should prove a priority for teachers and their continuous professional development. If we get it right, it offers us 50,000 small but essential solutions to the complex challenges of school.

Important questions need to be addressed before we undertake any departmental or whole-school initiative, such as:

● What problem are we solving? Are teachers clear about the 'what' and the 'why' of vocabulary development?
● Can teachers and school leaders clearly define the 'who', 'what', 'when' and 'where' of any vocabulary development programme?

- What support factors do teachers need to give the programme a chance of success (considering the necessities of time, tools and training)?
- What subject specific, or phase specific, support factors are required so that our initiative is appropriate to all teachers?
- How will we combine "faithful adoption with intelligent adaption"[6] so that our strategies best suit our school context?
- Are there realistic, practical time-scales to implement this programme?
- Have we considered how we will evaluate our programme from the start? How will we learn from the issues and roadblocks along the way and what will success look like when we get there?

Given vocabulary development can prove such a broad ranging facet of all teaching and learning, we should consider how the questions above are addressed in different ways by different individuals and groups in our schools. For a primary school that has many children who have come from homes with limited talk or support for reading, the emphasis will be, and should be, different to a secondary school that is looking to support high performing students to gain access to university.

An understanding of academic vocabulary explored in this book is relevant from three different, but inter-related perspectives: the individual teacher, departments or phase specific groups, and the whole school (see Figure 8.1).

Each chapter can be seen through one or more of these lenses. If an individual teacher lacks support on a whole school level, they can still apply many of the strategies and insights outlined in the previous chapters. A classroom charged with 'word consciousness' is within the reach of every teacher. Ideally though, we would be able to address

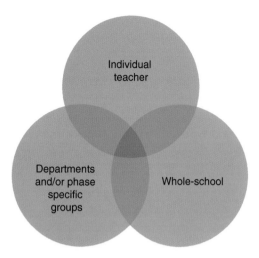

*Figure 8.1*   School perspectives on vocabulary development

the issue of the vocabulary gap with the collaborative support of school leadership. Given the integral role of word knowledge in our students' educational achievement, it is an issue for school leadership as much as it is a matter of teaching and learning.

## Breaking beyond the postcode prophesy

In drawing this book to a conclusion, inevitably we return to the evidence that academic success, and the breadth and depth of a child's vocabulary, are both inextricably linked with their home postcode, as well as the pay packet and qualifications of their parents.

The evidence is stark: children who are disadvantaged fall behind their more affluent peers by around two months for each year of secondary school. Recent research for the **Education Policy Institute** estimates "it would take around **50 years** for the disadvantage gap to close completely by the time pupils take their GCSEs".[7] We need to combat this depressing statistic with 50,000 solutions to bridge that cavernous 50-year gap.

I do not wish to reduce all the complexity of our education system to simply teaching vocabulary better, but it clearly proves a vital aspect of successful learning and so it is a good start. It is a problem we can define, understand and tackle successfully.

As teachers we cannot end social inequality or material poverty, but we can begin to make a difference in the classroom. We can help the word poor grow their vocabulary and become word rich. In helping children find their voice, thereby cracking the academic code of school, we offer the hope that every child can break beyond the boundaries of dismal postcode prophecies.

Back in 1651, the Welsh-born poet George Herbert shared a memorable proverb:

Good words are worth much but cost little.

As every good proverb should, these plain words offer every teacher sage guidance. It is our privilege to offer the children we teach a wealth of words. We should seize the opportunity and help to close the vocabulary gap.

## Notes

1  Binks-Cantrell, E., Washburn, E. K., Joshi, R. M., & Hougen, M. (2012). 'Peter effect in the preparation of reading teachers'. *Scientific Studies of Reading*, 16 (6): 526–536.
2  Berne, J. I., & Blachowich, C. L. Z. (2008). 'What reading teachers say about vocabulary instruction: Voices from the classroom'. *The Reading Teacher*, 62 (4): 314–323.
3  Cronbach, L. J. (1942). 'An analysis of techniques for diagnostic vocabulary testing'. *Journal of Educational Research*, 36 (3): 206–217.
4  Dale, E., & O'Rourke, J. (1976). *The living word vocabulary: The words we know, a national vocabulary inventory*. Elgin, IL: Dome.

5  Department for Education (2016). 'Standard for teachers' professional development'. Accessed online on 14 December 2017 at: www.gov.uk/government/publications/standard-for-teachers-professional-development.

6  This phrase is gratefully pinched from Dr Jonathan Sharples from the Education Endowment Foundation. It defines how we need to consistently follow agreed steps in the programme, but given we may need to make adaptations, either for subject disciplines or different groups of students.

7  Andrews, J., Robinson, D., & Hutchinson, J. (2017). *Closing the gap? Trends in educational attainment and disadvantage.* London: Education Policy Institute. Accessed online 20 August 2017 at: https://epi.org.uk/wp-content/uploads/2017/08/Closing-the-Gap_EPI.pdf.

# Appendix 1

## A list of common Latin loan words, or words with Latin roots, in the English language

1 *Acumen* – the ability to make good judgments.
2 *Ad hoc* – formed or done for a specific purpose as necessary.
3 *Ad nauseum* – referring to something repeated to the point of boredom.
4 *Agenda* – a list of things to be done.
5 *Altruism* – a selfless concern for others.
6 *Ambiguous* – having a double meaning or proving unclear.
7 *Atrocity* – a cruel act.
8 *Avarice* – greed.
9 *Bibulous* – to be excessively fond of drinking alcohol.
10 *Bona fide* – real; genuine.
11 *Caveat emptor* – let the buyer beware.
12 *Celibate* – to abstain from sex or marriage.
13 *Census* – a count of citizens.
14 *Chivalrous* (Fr.) – to be gallant.
15 *Circa* – approximately.
16 *Coitus interrputus* – interruption during sex.
17 *Condign* – fitting or worthy.
18 *Conglomerate* – a thing with numerous distinct parts that are grouped together.
19 *Compos mentis* – in control of one's own mind.

20 *Crepuscular* – pertaining to twilight.

21 *Cull* – to select from a variety of sources.

22 *Debilitate* – to weaken.

23 *De facto* – in fact; in reality.

24 *Ergo* – therefore.

25 *Erratum* – error.

26 *Et cetera* (etc.) – and the rest; and so on.

27 *Ex gratia* – with kindness, grace; no legal obligations.

28 *Ex libris* – from the books; from the library.

29 *Dirigible* – to prove capable of being guided.

30 *Facsimile* – an exact copy.

31 *Ferrous* – to be made of iron.

32 *Flux* – in the process of flowing.

33 *Futile* – in vain.

34 *Garrulity* – to be excessively talkative.

35 *Habeas corpus* – a court order instructing a person be brought before a judge.

36 *Impecunious* – to be poor.

37 *Incalculable* – too great to be counted.

38 *Incommunicado* (Sp.) – to not be in communication with others.

39 *Indefatigability* – to be tireless.

40 *In loco parentis* – to be in the place of the parent.

41 *Insipid* – to be lacking flavour.

42 *In situ* – in its original place.

43 *Introspection* – looking within at one's mental or emotional state.

44 *In vitro* – happening outside a living organism.

45 *Languid* – to be slow, relaxed.

46 *Lucubration* – writing, study or meditation.

47 *Malfeasance* (Fr.) – wrongdoing.

48 *Modicum* – a small amount.

49 *Moribund* – to be near death.

50 *Mundane* – to be lacking interest; or worldly as opposed to spiritual.

51  *Naive* – to exhibit a lack of experience.

52  *Obeisance* – to pay respect.

53  *Obvious* – clear (from the Latin for 'in the way').

54  *Parvenu* – a celebrity from obscure origins; an upstart.

55  *Per annum* – each year.

56  *Perpetuate* – to preserve, continue.

57  *Perturb* – to make anxious.

58  *Plausible* – probable.

59  *Precarious* – to be uncertain, or in an insecure position.

60  *Puerile* – to be childishly silly.

61  *Pulchritude* – beauty.

62  *Pusillanimity* – to show a lack of courage.

63  *Quid pro quo* – favours without expectation of return.

64  *Rapport* – a close relationship.

65  *Rapprochement* (Fr.) – to establish a harmonious relationship.

66  *Recalcitrant* – to be obstinate.

67  *Renegade* – a rebellious person.

68  *Reprisal* – retaliation.

69  *Sacrosanct* – to prove very important or holy and not to be messed with.

70  *Sine qua non* – essential; absolutely necessary.

71  *Simulacrum* – an image or representation of someone or something.

72  *Stipend* – a fixed allowance.

73  *Stultify* – to make appear foolish; cause to lose enthusiasm.

74  *Succumb* – to fail to resist.

75  *Taunt* (Fr.) – to provoke.

76  *Tentative* – provisional status; done without confidence.

77  *Terra firma* – dry land; the ground.

78  *Turpitude* – wicked or depraved character.

79  *Ubiquity* – to be found everywhere.

80  *Vice Versa* – the other way round.

# Appendix 2

## Latin roots related to the human body, people and groups

| Latin root | Meaning | Examples |
| --- | --- | --- |
| *Caput* | Head | Capital, capitulate, chapter |
| *Ora/os* | Mouth | Oral, oratory, osculation |
| *Dens* | Tooth | Dental, indenture, indentation |
| *Gaster* | Stomach | Gastric, gastronomy, gastropod |
| *Neuron* | Nerve | Neuron, neurosis, neurotic |
| *Manus* | Hand | Manual, manipulate, manoeuvre |
| *Ped/podos* | Foot | Pedestrian, arthropod, podium |
| *Derma* | Skin | Epidermis, hypodermic, taxidermy |
| *Carnem* | Flesh | Carnage, carnival, carnivore |
| *Oss* | Bone | Ossify, osteoporosis, ostracise |
| *Cor/cardia* | Heart | Concord, discord, courage |
| *Psyche* | Mind | Psychology, psychic, psychobabble |

| Latin root | Meaning | Examples |
| --- | --- | --- |
| *Anthropos* | Human | Anthropology, misanthrope, philanthropist |
| *Civis* | Citizen | Civil, civilian, uncivilised |
| *Demos* | People | Democracy, demagogue, demotic |
| *Ethnos* | People, race, tribe | Ethical, ethnic, ethnocentric |
| *Genus* | Race, kind, birth | Gender, genetic, genius, genre |
| *Populus* | People | Depopulate, Popular, population |
| *Socius* | Group | Social, society, sociopath |

# Appendix 3

## The 100 most commonly used words in the English language (from the 2.1 billion words in the Oxford English Corpus)

| 1–20 | 21–40 | 41–60 | 61–80 | 81–100 |
|---|---|---|---|---|
| 1. The | 21. This | 41. So | 61. People | 81. Back |
| 2. Be | 22. But | 42. Up | 62. Into | 82. After |
| 3. To | 23. His | 43. Out | 63. Year | 83. Use |
| 4. Of | 24. By | 44. If | 64. Your | 84. Two |
| 5. And | 25. From | 45. About | 65. Good | 85. How |
| 6. A | 26. They | 46. Who | 66. Some | 86. Our |
| 7. In | 27. We | 47. Get | 67. Could | 87. Work |
| 8. That | 28. Say | 48. Which | 68. Them | 88. First |
| 9. Have | 29. Her | 49. Go | 69. See | 89. Well |
| 10. I | 30. She | 50. Me | 70. Other | 90. Way |
| 11. It | 31. Or | 51. When | 71. Than | 91. Even |
| 12. For | 32. An | 52. Make | 72. Then | 92. New |
| 13. Not | 33. Will | 53. Can | 73. Now | 93. Want |
| 14. On | 34. My | 54. Like | 74. Look | 94. Because |
| 15. With | 35. One | 55. Time | 75. Only | 95. Any |
| 16. He | 36. All | 56. No | 76. Come | 96. These |
| 17. As | 37. Would | 57. Just | 77. Its | 97. Give |
| 18. You | 38. There | 58. Him | 78. Over | 98. Day |
| 19. Do | 39. Their | 59. Know | 79. Think | 99. Most |
| 20. At | 40. What | 60. Take | 80. Also | 100. Us |

# Appendix 4

## Avril Coxhead's full 570-word 'Academic Word List'

## Group 1

| | | | | | |
|---|---|---|---|---|---|
| analyse | approach | area | assess | assume | authority |
| available | benefit | concept | consist | constitute | context |
| contract | create | data | define | derive | distribute |
| economy | environment | establish | estimate | evident | export |
| factor | finance | formula | function | identify | income |
| indicate | individual | interpret | involve | issue | labour |
| legal | legislate | major | method | occur | percent |
| period | policy | principle | proceed | process | require |
| research | respond | role | section | sector | significant |
| similar | source | specific | structure | theory | vary |

## Group 2

| | | | | | |
|---|---|---|---|---|---|
| achieve | acquire | administrate | affect | appropriate | aspect |
| assist | category | chapter | commission | community | complex |
| compute | conclude | conduct | consequent | construct | consume |
| credit | culture | design | distinct | element | equate |
| evaluate | feature | final | focus | impact | injure |
| institute | invest | item | journal | maintain | normal |
| obtain | participate | perceive | positive | potential | previous |
| primary | purchase | range | region | regulate | relevant |
| reside | resource | restrict | secure | seek | select |
| site | strategy | survey | text | tradition | transfer |

## Appendix 4

## Group 3

| | | | | | |
|---|---|---|---|---|---|
| alternative | circumstance | comment | compensate | component | consent |
| considerable | constant | constrain | contribute | convene | coordinate |
| core | corporate | correspond | criteria | deduce | demonstrate |
| document | dominate | emphasis | ensure | exclude | framework |
| fund | illustrate | immigrate | imply | initial | instance |
| interact | justify | layer | link | locate | maximise |
| minor | negate | outcome | partner | philosophy | physical |
| proportion | publish | react | register | rely | remove |
| scheme | sequence | sex | shift | specify | sufficient |
| task | technical | technique | technology | valid | volume |

## Group 4

| | | | | | |
|---|---|---|---|---|---|
| access | adequate | annual | apparent | approximate | attitude |
| attribute | civil | code | commit | communicate | concentrate |
| confer | contrast | cycle | debate | despite | dimension |
| domestic | emerge | error | ethnic | goal | grant |
| hence | hypothesis | implement | implicate | impose | integrate |
| internal | investigate | job | label | mechanism | obvious |
| occupy | option | output | overall | parallel | parameter |
| phase | predict | principal | prior | professional | project |
| promote | regime | resolve | retain | series | statistic |
| status | stress | subsequent | sum | summary | undertake |

## Group 5

| | | | | | |
|---|---|---|---|---|---|
| academy | adjust | alter | amend | aware | capacity |
| challenge | clause | compound | conflict | consult | contact |
| decline | discrete | draft | enable | energy | enforce |
| entity | equivalent | evolve | expand | expose | external |
| facilitate | fundamental | generate | generation | image | liberal |
| licence | logic | margin | medical | mental | modify |
| monitor | network | notion | objective | orient | perspective |
| precise | prime | psychology | pursue | ratio | reject |
| revenue | stable | style | substitute | sustain | symbol |
| target | transit | trend | version | welfare | whereas |

# Group 6

| | | | | | |
|---|---|---|---|---|---|
| abstract | accurate | acknowledge | aggregate | allocate | assign |
| attach | author | bond | brief | capable | cite |
| cooperate | discriminate | display | diverse | domain | edit |
| enhance | estate | exceed | expert | explicit | federal |
| fee | flexible | furthermore | gender | ignorance | incentive |
| incidence | incorporate | index | inhibit | initiate | input |
| instruct | intelligence | interval | lecture | migrate | minimum |
| ministry | motive | neutral | nevertheless | overseas | precede |
| presume | rational | recover | reveal | scope | subsidy |
| tape | trace | transform | transport | underlie | utilise |

# Group 7

| | | | | | |
|---|---|---|---|---|---|
| adapt | adult | advocate | aid | channel | chemical |
| classic | comprehensive | comprise | confirm | contrary | convert |
| couple | decade | definite | deny | differentiate | dispose |
| dynamic | eliminate | empirical | equip | extract | file |
| finite | foundation | globe | grade | guarantee | hierarchy |
| identical | ideology | infer | innovate | insert | intervene |
| isolate | media | mode | paradigm | phenomenon | priority |
| prohibit | publication | quote | release | reverse | simulate |
| sole | somewhat | submit | successor | survive | thesis |
| topic | transmit | ultimate | unique | visible | voluntary |

# Group 8

| | | | | | |
|---|---|---|---|---|---|
| abandon | accompany | accumulate | ambiguous | append | appreciate |
| arbitrary | automate | bias | chart | clarify | commodity |
| complement | conform | contemporary | contradict | crucial | currency |
| denote | detect | deviate | displace | drama | eventual |
| exhibit | exploit | fluctuate | guideline | highlight | implicit |
| induce | inevitable | infrastructure | inspect | intense | manipulate |
| minimise | nuclear | offset | paragraph | plus | practitioner |
| predominant | prospect | radical | random | reinforce | restore |
| revise | schedule | tense | terminate | theme | thereby |
| uniform | vehicle | via | virtual | visual | widespread |

## Appendix 4

## *Group 9*

| | | | | | |
|---|---|---|---|---|---|
| accommodate | analogy | anticipate | assure | attain | behalf |
| bulk | cease | coherent | coincide | commence | compatible |
| concurrent | confine | controversy | converse | device | devote |
| diminish | distort | duration | erode | ethic | format |
| found | inherent | insight | integral | intermediate | manual |
| mature | mediate | medium | military | minimal | mutual |
| norm | overlap | passive | portion | preliminary | protocol |
| qualitative | refine | relax | restrain | revolution | rigid |
| route | scenario | sphere | subordinate | supplement | suspend |
| team | temporary | trigger | unify | violate | vision |

## *Group 10*

| | | | | | |
|---|---|---|---|---|---|
| adjacent | albeit | assemble | collapse | colleague | compile |
| conceive | convince | depress | encounter | enormous | forthcoming |
| incline | integrity | intrinsic | invoke | levy | likewise |
| nonetheless | notwithstanding | odd | ongoing | panel | persist |
| pose | reluctance | so-called | straightforward | undergo | whereby |

# Bibliography

Alderman, G. L., & Green, S. K. (2011). 'Fostering lifelong spellers through meaningful experiences'. *The Reading Teacher*, 64: 599–605. doi:10.1598/RT.64.8.5.

Andrews, J., Robinson, D., & Hutchinson, J. (2017). *Closing the gap? Trends in educational attainment and disadvantage.* London: Education Policy Institute. Accessed online 20 August 2017 at: https://epi.org.uk/wp-content/uploads/2017/08/Closing-the-Gap_EPI.pdf.

Astor, G.(1994). *June 6, 1944: The voices of D-Day.* New York, NY: St Martin's Press.

Baker, L. (2002). 'Metacognition in comprehension instruction'. In C. C. Block & M. Pressley (eds.), *Comprehension instruction: Research-based best practices* (pp. 77–95). New York, NY: Guilford.

Barton, G. (2013). *Don't call it literacy! What every teacher needs to know about speaking, listening, reading and writing.* London: Routledge.

Beck, I., McKeown, M., & Kucan, L. (2002). *Bringing words to life.* New York, NY: Guilford.

Benjamin, A. (2017). *Infusing vocabulary into the reading-writing workshop: A guide for teachers in grades K–8.* New York, NY: Routledge.

Berne, J. I., & Blachowich, C. L. Z. (2008). 'What reading teachers say about vocabulary instruction: Voices from the classroom'. *The Reading Teacher*, 62 (4): 314–323.

Biemiller, A. (2001). 'Teaching vocabulary'. *American Educator*, Spring: 24–28.

Biemiller, A. (2012). 'Teaching vocabulary in the primary grades: Vocabulary instruction needed'. In E. J. Kame'enui & J. F. Baumann (eds.), *Vocabulary instruction: Research to practice* (2nd ed.) (pp. 34–50). New York, NY: Guilford Press.

# Bibliography

Biemiller, A., &. Boote, C. (2006). 'An effective method for building meaning vocabulary in primary grades'. *Journal of Educational Psychology*, 98: 44–62. doi:10.1037/0022-0663.98.1.44.

Binks-Cantrell, E., Washburn, E. K., Joshi, R. M., & Hougen, M. (2012). 'Peter effect in the preparation of reading teachers'. *Scientific Studies of Reading*, 16 (6): 526–536.

Blachowicz, C., & Fisher, P. (2005). *Teaching vocabulary in all classrooms* (3rd ed.). New York, NY: Pearson Education.

Bowers, J.S., & Bowers, P. N. (2017). 'Beyond phonics: The case for teaching children the logic of the spelling system'. *Educational Psychologist*, 52 (2): 124–141.

Britton, J. (1970). *Language and learning*. Coral Gables, FL: University of Miami Press.

Butler, S., Urrutia, K., Buenger, A., Gonzalez, N., Hunt, M., & Eisenhart, C. (2010). 'A review of the current research on vocabulary instruction'. *National Reading Technical Assistance Program, 1*. Washington, DC: National Reading Technical Assistance Center.

Cain, K., & Oakhill, J. (2011). 'Matthew effects in young readers: Reading comprehension and reading experience aid vocabulary development'. *Journal of Learning Disabilities*, 44 (5): 431–443. doi:10.1177/0022219411410042.

Carlisle, J. F. (2010). 'Effects of instruction in morphological awareness on literacy achievement: An integrative review'. *Reading Research Quarterly*, 45: 464–487. doi:10.1598/RRQ.45.4.5.

Carrier, S. J. (2011). 'Effective strategies for teaching science vocabulary'. Learn NC. Accessed online on 10 September 2016 at: www.learnnc.org/lp/pages/7079?ref=searchwww.learnnc.org/lp/pages/7079?ref=search.

Carter, R., & McCarthy, M. (2006). *Cambridge grammar of English: A comprehensive guide: Written and spoken English*. Cambridge: Cambridge University Press.

Childs, P. E., Markic, S., & Ryan, M. C. (2015). 'The role of language in the teaching and learning of chemistry'. In J. García-Martínez & E. Serrano-Torregrosa (eds.), *Chemistry education: Best practices, opportunities and trends* (pp. 421–446). Weinheim: Wiley-VCH Verlag GmbH & Co.

Clemens, N. H., Ragan, K., & Widales-Benitez, O. (2016). 'Reading difficulties in young children: Beyond basic early literacy skills'. *Policy Insights from the Behavioral and Brain Sciences*, 3 (2): 177–184.

Connor, C. M., Piasta, S. B., Fishman, B., Glasney, S., Schatschneider, C., Crowe, E., Underwood, P., & Morrison, F. J. (2009). 'Individualizing student instruction precisely: Effects of Child x Instruction interactions on first graders' literacy development'. *Child Development Journal*, 80 (1): 77–100. doi: 10.1111/j.1467-8624.2008.01247.x.

Coxhead, A. (2000). 'A new academic word list'. *TESOL Quarterly*, 34 (2): 213–238.

Cronbach, L. J. (1942). 'An analysis of techniques for diagnostic vocabulary testing'. *Journal of Educational Research*, 36 (3): 206–217.

Crystal, D. (2007). *Words, words, words*. New York, NY: Oxford University Press.

Crystal, D. (2011). *The story of English in 100 words*. London: Profile Books.

Crystal, D. (2012). *Spell it out: The singular story of English spelling*. London: Profile Books.

Cunningham, A. E. (2005). 'Vocabulary growth through independent reading and reading aloud to children'. In E. H. Hiebert & M. L. Kamhi (eds.), *Teaching and learning vocabulary: Bringing research to practice* (pp. 45–68). Mahwah, NJ: Lawrence Erlbaum Associates.

Cunningham, A. E., & Stanovich, K. E. (1997). 'Early reading acquisition and its relation to reading experience and ability 10 years later'. *Developmental Psychology*, 33: 934–945.

Cunningham, A. E., & Stanovich, K. E. (1998). 'What reading does for the mind'. *American Educator*, 22 (1–2): 8–15.

Dale, E., & O'Rourke, J. (1976). *The living word vocabulary: The words we know, a national vocabulary inventory*. Elgin, IL: Dome.

Department for Education (2009). *The national strategies: 'Support for spelling'* (2nd ed.). Accessible online on 14 December 2017 at: http://webarchive.nationalarchives.gov.uk/20110813013929/http:// teachingandlearningresources.org.uk/collection/35326.

Department for Education (2016). 'Standard for teachers' professional development'. Accessed online on 14 December 2017 at: www.gov. uk/government/publications/standard-for-teachers-professional-development.

Department of Education, UK Government (2016). *The way of the Dodo*. London: Department of Education.

Dougherty Stahl, K. A., & Bravo, M. A. (2010). 'Contemporary classroom vocabulary assessment for content areas'. *The Reading Teacher*, 63 (7): 566–578.

Dunston, P. J., & Tyminski, A. M. (2013). 'What's the big deal about vocabulary?' *NCTM, Mathematics Teaching in the Middle School*, 19 (1): 38–45.

Education Endowment Foundation (14 July 2016). 'Texting parents about tests and homework can improve maths results and reduce absenteeism'. Accessed online on 10 August 2017 at: https:// educationendowmentfoundation.org.uk/news/texting-parents-about-tests-and-homework-can-improve-maths-results-and-redu/.

Education Endowment Foundation (2017a). *Improving literacy in key stage one*. London: Education Endowment Foundation.

# Bibliography

Education Endowment Foundation (2017b). *Improving literacy in key stage two: Guidance report*. London: Education Endowment Foundation.

Education Endowment Foundation and the University of Oxford (2017). *Review of SES and science learning in formal educational settings: A report prepared for the EEF and the Royal Society*. London: Education Endowment Foundation. Accessed online on 27 September 2017 at: https://educationendowmentfoundation.org.uk/public/files/Review_of_SES_and_Science_Learning_in_Formal_Educational_Settings.pdf.

Elleman, A., Linda, E., Morphy, P., & Compton, D. (2009). 'The impact of vocabulary instruction on passage level comprehension of school-age children: A meta-analysis'. *Journal of Educational Effectiveness*, 2: 1–44.

Eunice Kennedy Shriver National Institute of Child Health and Human Development, NIH, DHHS. (2010). *What content-area teachers should know about adolescent literacy*. Washington, DC: U.S. Government Printing Office.

Firth, J. R. (1957). *Papers in linguistics*. Oxford: Oxford University Press.

Gardner, D. (2013). *Exploring vocabulary: Language in action*. London: Routledge.

Genesee, F., Lindholm-Leary, K., Saunders, W., & Christian, D. (2006). *Educating English language learners: A synthesis of research evidence*. Cambridge: Cambridge University Press.

Grabe, W. (2009). *Reading in a second language: Moving from theory to practice*. New York, NY: Cambridge University Press.

Graesser, A. C., & Person, N. K. (1994). 'Question asking during tutoring'. *American Education Research Journal*, 31 (1): 104–137.

Graham, S. (1999). 'Handwriting and spelling instruction for students with learning disabilities: A review'. *Learning Disability Quarterly*, 22 (2): 78–98.

Graham, S., & Perin, D. (2007). 'A meta-analysis of writing instruction for adolescent students'. *Journal of Educational Psychology*, 99 (3): 445–476. doi:10.1037/0022-0663.99.3.445.

Graves, M. F. (1986). 'Chapter 2: Vocabulary learning and instruction'. *Review of Research in Education*, 13 (1): 49–89.

Graves, M. F. (2005). *The vocabulary book: Learning and instruction (language and literacy series)*. New York, NY: Teachers College Press.

Graves, M., & Hammond, H. K. (1980). 'A validated procedure for teaching prefixes and its effect on students' ability to assign meanings to novel words'. In M. Kamil and A. Moe (eds.), *Perspectives on reading research and instruction* (pp. 184–188). Washington, DC: National Reading Conference.

Green, T. M. (2008). *The Greek and Latin roots of English* (4th ed.). Lanham, MD: Rowman & Littlefield.

Guthrie, J. T., Wigfield, A., & Klauda, S. L. (2012). 'Adolescents' engagement in academic literacy' (Report No. 7). Accessed online on 15 July 2017 at: www.corilearning.com/research-publications.

Hanson, S., & Padua, J. F. M. (2016). 'Teaching vocabulary explicitly, Pacific resources for education'. Accessed online on 12 September 2016 at: http://prel.org/wp-content/uploads/2014/06/vocabulary_lo_res.pdf.

Hart, B., & Risley, T. R. (1995). *Meaningful differences in the everyday experiences of young American children: The everyday experience of one and two-year-old American children.* Baltimore, MD: Paul H. Brookes.

Hattie, J., & Yates, G. C. R. (2014). *Visible learning and the science of how we learn.* London: Routledge.

Hickey, P. J., & Lewis, T. (2015). 'To win the game, know the rules and legitimise the players: Disciplinary literacy and multilingual learners'. *The Language and Literacy Spectrum,* 25: 18–28.

Hirsch Jr, E. D. (2000). 'You can always look it up—or can you?' *American Educator,* 24 (1): 4–9.

Hirsch Jr, E. D. (2003). 'Reading comprehension requires knowledge—of words and the world'. *American Educator,* 27 (1): 10–13.

Hirsch Jr, E. D. (2013). 'A wealth of words. The key to increasing upward mobility is expanding vocabulary'. *City Journal,* 23 (1). Accessed online on 20 October 2016 at: www.city-journal.org/html/wealth-words-13523.html.

Hirsch Jr, E. D., & Moats, L. C. (2001). 'Overcoming the language gap'. *American Educator,* 25 (2): 4–9.

Holmes-Henderson, A. (2016). 'Teaching Latin and Greek in primary classrooms: The Classics in Communities project'. *Journal of Classics Teaching,* 17 (33): 50–53.

Horowitz, R., & Samuels, S. J., (2017). *The achievement gap in reading: Complex causes, persistent issues, possible solutions.* New York, NY: Routledge.

Jackson, P. (30 March 2011). '100 words of English: How far can it get you?' BBC News website. Accessed online on 6 June 2016 at: http://www.bbc.co.uk/news/magazine-12894638.

Jetton, T. L., & Shanahan, C. (2012). *Adolescent literacy in the academic disciplines.* New York, NY: Guildford Press.

Jones, B. R., Hopper, P. F., & Franz, D. P. (2008). 'Mathematics: A second language'. *Mathematics Teacher,* 102 (4): 307–312.

Kafka, F. (Translation, 2007). *Metamorphosis and other stories.* London: Penguin Books.

Kame'enui, E. J., & Baumann, J. F. (eds.). (2012). *Vocabulary instruction: Research to practice.* New York, NY: Guilford Press.

# Bibliography

Kirby, J. R., & Bowers, P. N. (2012). 'Morphology works. Ontario Ministry of Education Literacy and Numeracy Secretariat, what works?' *Research in Practice*, 41: 1–4.

Krashen, S. (1989). 'We acquire vocabulary and spelling by reading: Additional evidence for the input hypothesis'. *The Modern Language Journal*, 73 (4): 440–464.

Laufer, B. (2017). 'From word parts to full texts: Searching for effective methods of vocabulary learning'. *Language Teaching Research*, 21 (1): 5–11. doi:10.1177/1362168816683118.

Law, J., Rush, R., Schoon, I., & Parsons, S. (2009). 'Modeling developmental language difficulties from school entry into adulthood: Literacy, mental health, and employment outcomes'. *Journal of Speech, Language and Hearing Research*, 52 (6): 1401–1416.

Lemov, D., Driggs, C., & Woolway, E. (2016). *Reading reconsidered: A practical guide to rigorous literacy instruction*. San Francisco, CA: Jossey-Bass.

McCutchen, D., Harry, D. R., Cox, S., Sidman, S. Covill, E. A., & Cunningham, A. E. (2002). 'Reading teachers' knowledge of children's literature and English phonology'. *Annals of Dyslexia*, 52 (1): 205–228.

McKay, S. (26 August 2010). 'Telegraph crossword: Cracking hobby won the day – The boffins of Bletchley cut their teeth on the Telegraph crossword'. *The Telegraph*. Accessed online on 14 December 2017 at: www.telegraph.co.uk/lifestyle/wellbeing/7966268/Telegraph-cross word-Cracking-hobby-won-the-day.html.

Marchman, V. A., & Fernald, A. (2008). 'Speed of word recognition and vocabulary knowledge in infancy predict cognitive and language outcomes in later childhood'. *Developmental Science*, 11: F9–F16.

Massaro, D. W. (2016). 'Two different communication genres and implications for vocabulary development and learning to read'. *Journal of Literacy Research*, 47 (4): 505–527.

Menke, D., & Pressley, M. (1994). 'Elaborative interrogation: Using "why" questions to enhance the learning from text'. *Journal of Reading*, 37 (8): 642–645.

Merrell, C., & Tymms, P. (2007). 'Identifying reading problems with computer-adaptive assessments. Journal of Computer Assisted Learning'. *Journal of Computer Assisted Learning*, 23: 27–35. doi:10.1111/j.1365-2729.2007.00196.x.

Moats, L. (1999). 'Reading is like rocket science: What expert teachers of reading should know and be able to do'. Washington, DC: The American Federation of Teachers. Accessed online on 12 December 2015 at: www.ldaustralia.org/client/documents/Teaching%20Reading%20is%20Rocket%20Science%20-%20Moats.pdf.

Moats, L. C. (2005). 'How spelling supports reading: And why is more regular and predictable than you might think'. *American Educator*,

6 (12–22): 42–43. Accessed online on 7 May 2014 at: www.aft.org/sites/default/files/periodicals/Moats.pdf.

Montgomery, S. L. (1996). *The scientific voice.* New York, NY: Guilford Press.

Murphy, V. A. (2015). 'A systematic review of intervention research examining English language and literacy development in children with English as an Additional Language (EAL)'. Commissioned by the Education Endowment Foundation. Accessed online on 5 November 2016 at: https://educationendowmentfoundation.org.uk/public/files/Publications/EAL_Systematic_review.pdf.

Nagy, W. E., & Anderson, R. (1984). 'How many words are there in printed school English?'. *Reading Research Quarterly,* 19: 304–330.

Nagy, W. E., & Herman, P. A. (1987). 'Breadth and depth of vocabulary knowledge: Implications for acquisition and instruction'. In M. McKeown & M. Curtis (eds.), *The nature of vocabulary acquisition* (pp. 19–35). Hillside, NJ: Lawrence Erlbaum Associates.

Nagy, W. E., & Townsend, D. (2012). 'Words as tools: Learning academic vocabulary as language acquisition'. *Reading Research Quarterly,* 47 (1): 91–108. doi:10.1002/RRQ.011.

Nagy, W. E., Berninger V. W., & Abbott R. D. (2006). 'Contributions of morphology beyond phonology to literacy outcomes of upper elementary and middle-school students'. *Journal of Educational Psychology,* 98: 134–147.

Nation, K. (2005). 'Children's reading comprehension difficulties'. In M. J. Snowling and C. Hulme (eds.), *The science of reading: A handbook* (pp. 248–265). Oxford: Blackwell Publishing Ltd. doi:10.1002/9780470757642.ch14.

Nation, K. (2017). 'Nurturing a lexical legacy: Reading experience is critical for the development of word reading skill'. *NPJ Science of Learning,* 2 (1): 3. doi:10.1038/s41539-017-0004-7.

National Institute of Child Health and Human Development (2000). *Report of the National Reading Panel. Teaching children to read: An evidence-based assessment of the scientific research literature on reading and its implications for reading instruction* (NIH Publication No. 00-4769). Washington, DC: U.S. Government Printing Office.

Nuthall, G. (2007). *The hidden lives of learners.* Wellington: NZCER Press.

Oakhill, J., Cain, K., & Elbro, C. (2014). *Understanding and teaching reading comprehension: A handbook.* London: Routledge.

O'Halloran, K. L. (2005) (Reprinted 2008). *Mathematical discourse: Language, symbolism and visual images.* London and New York, NY: Continuum.

O'Keefe, A., Carter, R., & McCarthy, M. (2007). *From corpus to classroom: language use and language teaching.* Cambridge: Cambridge

University Press. Accessed online on 5 May 2017 at: http://npu.edu. ua/!e-book/book/djvu/A/iif_kgpm_OKeefee.%20FCTC.pdf.

Olson, R. K., Keenan, J. M., Byrne, B., Samuelsson, S., Coventry, W. L., Corley, R., Wadsworth, S. J., Willcutt, E. G., DeFries, J. C., Pennington, B. F., & Hulslander, J. (2007). 'Genetic and environmental influences on vocabulary and reading development'. *Scientific Studies of Reading: The Official Journal of the Society for the Scientific Study of Reading*, 20 (1–2): 51–75. doi:10.1007/s11145-006-9018-x.

Orwell, G. (1949). *1984*. London: Penguin Books.

Osborne, J., & Dillon, J. (2010). *Good practice in science teaching: What research has to say*. New York, NY: Open University Press.

Ouellette, G. P. (2006). 'What's meaning got to do with it: The role of vocabulary in word reading and reading comprehension'. *Journal of Educational Psychology*, 98 (3): 554–566.

Oxford Dictionary (2017). Oxford: Oxford University Press.

Perfetti, C. A., & Hart, L. (2002). 'The lexical quality hypothesis'. In L. Verhoeven (ed.), *Precursors of functional literacy* (pp. 189–213). Philadelphia, PA: John Benjamins.

Podhajski, B., Mather, N., Nathan, J., & Sammons, J. (2009). 'Professional development in scientifically based reading instruction: Teacher knowledge and reading outcomes'. *Journal of Learning Disabilities*, 42 (5): 403–417. doi: 10.1177/0022219409338737.

Priestley, J. B. (Reprinted in 2000). *An inspector calls and other plays*. Penguin: London.

Rasinski, T., Samuels, S. J., Hiebert, E., Petscher, Y., & Feller, K. (2011). 'The relationship between a silent reading fluency instructional protocol on students' reading comprehension and achievement in an urban school setting'. *Reading Psychology*, 32 (1): 75–97.

Reed, D. K. (2008). 'A synthesis of morphology interventions and effects on reading outcomes for students in grades K–12'. *Learning Disabilities Research and Practice*, 23: 36–49. doi:10.1111/j.1540-5826. 2007.00261.x.

Reisman, A. (2012). 'Reading like a historian: A document-based history curriculum intervention in urban high schools'. *Cognition and Instruction*, 30 (1): 86–112.

Rowe, M. B. (1987). 'Wait time: Slowing down may be a way of speeding up'. *American Educator*, 11 (Spring): 38–47.

Saunders, M., Goldenberg, C., & Marcelletti, D. (2013). 'English language development: Guidelines for instruction'. *American Educator*, Summer: 13–39

Scarborough, H. S. (2001). 'Connecting early language and literacy to later reading (dis)abilities: Evidence, theory, and practice'. In S. Neuman & D. Dickinson (eds.), *Handbook for research in early literacy* (pp. 97–110). New York, NY: Guilford Press.

Schleppegrell, M. J. (2007). 'The linguistic challenges of mathematics teaching and learning: A research review'. *Reading and Writing Quarterly*, 23 (2): 139–159.

Schmitt, N., & Pellicer-Sánchez, A. (2010). 'Incidental vocabulary acquisition from an authentic novel: *Do things fall apart?*' *Reading in a Foreign Language*, 22 (1): 31–55

Scott, J. A., & Nagy, W. E. (1997). 'Understanding the definitions of unfamiliar verbs'. *Reading Research Quarterly*, 32 (2): 184–200.

Sedita, J. (2005). 'Effective vocabulary instruction. *Insights on Learning Disabilities*, 2 (1): 33–45.

Seidenberg, M. (2017). *Language at the speed of sight: Why we read, why so many can't and what we can do about it.* New York, NY: Basic Books.

Shanahan, T., & Barr, R. (1995). 'Reading recovery: An independent evaluation of the effects of an early instructional intervention for at risk learners'. *Reading Research Quarterly*, 30 (4): 958–996.

Shanahan, T., & Shanahan, C. (2008). 'Teaching disciplinary literacy to adolescents: Rethinking content-area literacy'. *Harvard Educational Review*, 78 (1): 40–59.

Snow, C. E., & Beals, D. E. (2006). 'Mealtime talk that supports literacy development'. *New Directions for Child and Adolescent Development*, Spring (111): 51–66.

Spencer, S., Clegg, J., & Stackhouse, J. (2012). 'Language and disadvantage: A comparison of the language abilities of adolescents from two different socioeconomic areas'. *International Journal of Language and Communication Disorders*, 47: 274–284. doi: 10.1111/j.1460-6984.2011. 00104x.

Spencer, S., Clegg, J., Stackhouse, J., & Rush, R. (2017). 'Contribution of spoken language and socio-economic background to adolescents' educational achievement at aged 16 years'. *International Journal of Language Disorders*, 52: 184–196. doi: 10.1111/1460-6984.12264.

Stahl, S. A. (1999). *Vocabulary development.* Cambridge, MA: Brookline Books.

Stanovich, K. E. (1986). 'Mathew effects in reading: Some consequences of individual differences in the acquisition of literacy'. *Reading Research Quarterly*, 21: 360–407.

Tao, P. K. (1994). 'Words that matter in science: A study of Hong Kong students' comprehension of non-technical words in science'. *Educational Research Journal*, 9 (1): 15–23.

Teaching School Council (2017). 'Modern foreign languages pedagogy review: A review of modern foreign languages teaching practice in key stage two and key stage three'. Accessed online on 10 August 2017 at: www.tscouncil.org.uk/wp-content/uploads/2016/12/MFL-Pedagogy-Review-Report-2.pdf.

## Bibliography

Treffers-Daller, J., & Milton, J. (2013). 'Vocabulary size revisited: The link between vocabulary size and academic achievement'. *Applied Linguistics Review*, 4 (1): 151–172. doi: 10.1515/applirev-2013-0007.

Ward, H. (24 May 2016). TES online. 'Try the SATs reading paper that left pupils in tears'. Accessed online on 27 May 2016 at: www.tes.com/news/school-news/breaking-news/try-sats-reading-paper-left-pupils-tears.

Wexler, J., Mitchell, M. A., Clancy, E. E., & Silverman, R. D. (2016). 'An investigation of literacy practices in high school science classrooms'. *Reading and Writing Quarterly*, 33 (3): 258–277.

White, T. G., Sowell, J., & Yanagihara, A. (1989). 'Teaching elementary students to use word part clues'. *The Reading Teacher*, 42: 302–308.

Willingham, D. T. (2009). *Why don't students like school?* San Francisco, CA: Jossey Bass.

Willingham, D. T. (2017). *The reading mind: A cognitive approach to understanding how the mind reads.* San Francisco, CA: Jossey Bass.

Winch, G., Johnston, R. R., March, P., Ljungdahl, L., & Holliday, M. (2010). *Literacy: Reading, writing and children's literature* (4th ed.). South Melbourne: Oxford University Press.

Wolsey, T. D., & Lapp, D. (2017). *Literacy in the disciplines: A teacher's guide for grades 5–12.* New York, NY: The Guilford Press.

# Index

Index

# Index

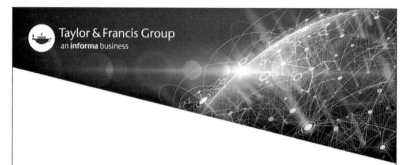

Printed in Great Britain
by Amazon